The Humble Giant

The Humble Giant

Moses Coady,
Canada's Rural Revolutionary

Jim Lotz

NOVALIS

Cover design: Blair Turner
Cover image:© Yousef Karsh / Retna Ltd.
Interior images: Courtesy of St. Francis Xavier University Archives
Layout: Caroline Galhidi

Business Office:
Novalis
49 Front Street East, 2nd Floor
Toronto, Ontario, Canada
M5E 1B3

Phone: 1-800-387-7164
Fax: 1-800-204-4140
E-mail: cservice@novalis-inc.com
www.novalis.ca

Library and Archives Canada Cataloguing in Publication

Lotz, Jim, 1929–
    The humble giant : Moses Coady, Canada's rural
revolutionary / Jim Lotz.

Includes bibliographical references.
ISBN 2-89507-668-5

    1. Coady, M. M. (Moses Michael), 1882-1959. 2. Antigonish
movement. 3. Cooperation--Biography. 4. Social reformers-
Nova Scotia--Biography. 5. Catholic Church--Clergy--Biography.
6. Clergy--Nova Scotia--Biography. I. Title.

LB775.C56L68 2005   334'.092   C2005-904528-0

Printed in Canada.

We acknowledge the financial support of the Government of Canada through the Book
Publishing Industry Development Program (BPIDP) for our publishing activities.

5 4 3 2 1   09 08 07 06 05

Dedicated, with affection and respect, to
Father Joseph Brossard, o.m.i.
and
Dr. Anthony Setsabi,
who keep the flame of the Antigonish Movement
burning brightly in Lesotho.

Contents

Preface

This book tells the story of an outstanding Canadian and the social movement he led. Father Moses Michael Coady had remarkable gifts of leadership, drawing around him a talented and dynamic band of followers, women and men, whom he called "noble souls." During the Great Depression, which began in 1929, they set out to rescue others from poverty, dependency and despair. Operating from the Extension Department of St. Francis Xavier (St. F.X.) University in eastern Nova Scotia, Coady's followers laid the foundations for the co-operative and credit union movements that now play a significant role in the social and economic life of people around the world.

Coady and his people did not view men and women as "hands" or "factors of production" or "human resources." They saw them as God's creation, imbued with potential for becoming fully human, with a divine spark that could be fanned into flame through adult education. As Coady put it, "We are not building credit unions. We are building men." Coady, ahead of his time in this as in so many other things, had the highest regard for women. He treated them as equals; gave them positions of power and encouraged them to develop their potential to the full.

Alex Laidlaw, associate director at the Extension Department, collected Coady's speeches and writings in *The Man from Margaree*. It appeared in 1971, twelve years after Coady died at the age of 77. Laidlaw wrote: "No book can recapture the restless, persistent Moses Coady; it can only record impressions and salvage some of his wisdom from dead files."

One writer called Moses Coady a "humble giant." This description captures the essence of this idealistic, practical leader who inspired so many people with his vision of the good and abundant life, yet always felt he had not done enough for them.

Two writers have produced biographies of him. In *Coady Remembered* (1985), Malcolm MacLellan, former president of St. F.X., presented his friend as a very human being, through anecdotes and personal recollections. If MacLellan put Coady on a pedestal, Dr. Michael Welton stretched him on a couch. *Little Mosie from the Margaree* (2001), a scholarly work, explores the intellectual and spiritual roots of the man. Welton claims that Coady created "a redemptive narrative" and that "his image of uneducated, simple, unsophisticated primary producers...and industrial workers running their own economic affairs turned out...to be mainly a beautiful fairy tale."

The present biography sets Coady and his work in the context of social movements. These, by their very nature, create expectations about better worlds that may never be realized. Myths – and even fairy tales – cluster around such movements, obscuring their reality. But they can inspire others to work towards better lives for themselves and others. We need myths and fairy tales that point to wonders and possibilities excluded from rational thought.

Coady grew up in the Margaree Valley in Cape Breton, hemmed in by mountains that are the edges of a plateau. Life there in the years before and after Coady was born in 1882 was simple and secure, but he travelled beyond the mountains. What he learned in other places complemented what he discovered from working on the land and from his family and friends. Coady knew how to touch the hearts and imaginations of ordinary men and women. He also showed them how to use their heads and their hands to become "Masters of Their Own Destiny," the title of the only book he wrote.

Coady's vision of a new society based on adult education and co-operative action did not come into being everywhere. But this is no reflection on that vision or on the way that Coady went about presenting it. If, like Moses in the Bible, he did not reach the Promised Land, he caught sight of the shape of it in the small collective ventures that his movement fostered.

I had the good fortune to know some of the people who worked with Coady or had met him. They shared their stories and memories of the man and the movement, and I am grateful to them. They include Zita Cameron, Sisters Marie Michael and Irene Doyle, Ellen Arsenault, Alex Laidlaw, J.D. Nelson MacDonald, Alex Sim, Russell Elliott, Des Connor, and Fred Walsh. The help provided by Kathy MacKenzie, senior archivist of St. Francis Xavier University, James Cameron, the university historian, and Michael Welton is much appreciated. As far as possible, I have let Coady tell his own story in his own words. Unless otherwise indicated, passages in this book in quotation marks are taken from his speeches and writings.

I am grateful for the encouragement of Kevin Burns, Commissioning Editor of Novalis, and for the meticulous editing of Bruce Henry.

What Moses Coady and his colleagues did would be known as community development these days. It bids fair to become the flavour of the millennium with its talk of decentralized activity and economic democracy. Coady and his people made these words flesh at a time when hope had fled. My research, teaching and involvement in community development have been enriched by Coady's words, ideas and actions and those of the people who worked with him. For this I am profoundly grateful, as are so many others who strive to follow the path that he blazed for us as we work towards a more egalitarian, just, human and creative world.

Jim Lotz

Halifax, Nova Scotia

September 2005

1

The Man from Margaree

He thought big, he talked big and he achieved great results.
There was nothing small about him.

—Malcolm MacLellan, *Coady Remembered*

The Cabot Trail loops around northern Cape Breton Island in Nova Scotia. For most of its length, the road snakes along the narrow margin between the ocean and the barren uplands of the island's interior. North of Baddeck, the highway passes through the Margaree Valley, a fertile area with a fish-filled river running through it. Cape Breton has few good farming areas. The Margaree is an exception, containing stretches of fine agricultural land. With hard work, the first settlers here created a good life for themselves, and built vibrant communities based on self-help and mutual aid.

From this remote and fruitful part of Canada came the leader of one of the most successful social action movements in the country's history. The Antigonish Movement, as it became known, showed fishermen, farmers and urban workers how to lift themselves out of poverty and dependency through their own efforts. People came from all over the world to learn how they did this. Each year, students from developing nations continue to visit the place that nurtured a great Canadian named Moses Michael Coady. What he did, and how he did it, is as relevant to our time as it was to his days of despair and lost hopes for a better world.

Moses Coady was born on January 3, 1882, in a house high up on the mountain overlooking the Margaree River. He was named for an ancestor on his mother's side who had led a company of United Irishmen in the rebellion of 1798. In later years, Coady added the middle name "Michael" to distinguish himself from other Coadys. The eldest son of Whistling Mick and Sarah, he grew up among pioneer stock who had made new lives in a new land. The people of the Margaree turned their hands to anything that offered some returns. As Coady put it, "We were carpenters, coopers, woodsmen, fishermen, farmers all in one…in the primeval forest of those early days." This hard world built up the young man's muscles: "This rugged life developed for me a great physique and the ability to endure long and sustained efforts."

Many parts of Cape Breton, settled by Highland Scots and Acadians who escaped the deportation of 1755, had homogenous cultures. The Margaree Valley had a more diverse population, made up of the first two groups, as well as English and Irish settlers and some from United Empire Loyalist stock. They worked from dawn to dusk, helping each other to survive and thrive. Coady's father became a local leader. His son described Whistling Mick as a "lion of a man [who] whistled through life while he thought out new schemes of progress in those hard old days when progress was difficult. Without question, my father was an outstanding man."

A belief in progress and ways to achieve it formed part of the legacy Coady received from his father. From him and others like him, the young man acquired other values that would serve him well in later years. These people were "men of tremendous physique and courage … fighters for impossible causes." Coady fought for successful causes: opportunities for the poor, social justice, economic democracy. And he was helped by other characteristics of the people with whom he grew up, celebrating "their imagination, their wonder and their impatience [and] tremendous pull to the unseen, the unknown and the things that needed to be done." He could have been describing himself.

Whistling Mick had strong entrepreneurial instincts. Two years after the birth of his first son, Moses, he bought a 260-hectare (650-acre) mixed farm about six kilometres from Margaree Centre, the biggest community in the valley.

As well as running a farm, Coady's father fished, worked in the woods and earned money as a contractor, carpenter and coffin maker.

Tall, good-looking and pious, Whistling Mick established himself as a respected member of the community. He tried his hand at money-lending, a venture that proved unsuccessful and may have impressed his son with the importance of paying careful attention to cash flows and capital accumulation. Coady makes no mention of his mother, Sarah, in his writings, but she no doubt had a strong influence on him.

Coady describes his birthplace and the valley where he lived until he was 23 years old as "the two beauty spots of a community that for scenery, in the estimation of travellers, ranks with the best in the world." This lovely land loomed forever in his imagination as his Shangri-La, his utopia, his land of lost content where people lived in harmony with each other and their environment.

The small community of the Margaree shaped the way Coady saw the world when he was an adult and wandered away from his home. People there cared for each other, shared what they had. Coady grew up in a large kinship system made up of Coadys and Tompkinses. Sarah had twelve robust children; the family also took into their home a sickly nephew, James Tompkins. Father Jimmy, as he became known in later life, played a prominent role in the life of his double cousin Moses, becoming his mentor and inspiration.

Like other youngsters, Coady fished and hunted and roamed the valley and the uplands that ringed it. He loved this place, but did not become a rural romantic. He knew how perilous and precarious life could be, describing the Margaree River as "a glorious enemy." When ice jammed its waters in the spring, the river overflowed its banks, drowning settlers and animals and flooding the fertile bottom lands along its shores. The river flows into the Gulf of St. Lawrence at Margaree Harbour. The coast here experiences strong southeast winds, the dreaded sûetes. Everyone huddles in their houses when these gales rip roofs from buildings and sink boats on this harsh coast. Three of Coady's ancestors drowned in a sudden squall that upset their boat in Margaree Harbour.

Coady loved to leave the settled, placid valley and head into the tree-clad mountains that surrounded it. This wild, forested land "fostered in me a love of faraway things and places that I knew only from half-forgotten tales, filled in by my imagination and dreams." In these solitudes, Coady turned into a visionary, forever peering into the future, striving to see beyond the physical and mental barriers that bound and limited the potential of his fellows. To others, he noted, a mountain was "a wall, a boundary separating those inside from those outside, making them different."

Combine a mountain "with imagination and wonder, it is a challenge and an exciting bridge to the wonderful world beyond." Coady loved challenges, and constantly sought bridges and passes through the mountains of despair that rose during the years in which he came to manhood. He found his own chosen path to take him beyond the barriers that hampered his ability to love and serve others. He stated, "If I have any creative imagination and a soul that tends to poetry and idealism, I owe it, I think, in large part to the natural beauty of the environment."

The waters of the Margaree River flow over granite, and are crystal clear throughout its 130-kilometre system. And so it was with Coady. He had granite in his soul: a rock-solid determination to change the lives of the poor people of eastern Nova Scotia for the better. He saw beauty and potential in places and people where others saw only barrenness and lack of promise. He sought to bend nature to his will in this undertaking. When he wandered in the woods, "the voice of the trees was always in my ears. Clean and strong and beautiful." He drew lessons from his travels, seeing forest growth that had "gone wild, a natural monopoly that in killing all around...had killed itself." These trees would have made fine furniture. They were "crying out to achieve their destiny."

Coady thought like a man of action and acted like a man of thought. Yet he had a mystical edge to his mind, a poetic soul nurtured by his life in the Margaree. The air here has a special quality. On some days, the sunlight, sharp and bright, makes every part of the landscape clear and the forested hills shine, brilliant in their greenery. In the fall, the trees turn scarlet, orange and gold as an ethereal blue haze softens the outlines of the land and its harsh edges. In winter, the fields lie silent and lovely under snow. In days gone by, the settlers relaxed, organized ceilidhs, played their fiddles, told stories and visited friends during the winter. With spring came new life as the ice left the Margaree River.

This valley strongly influenced Coady's thoughts and actions. Some parts of his life are clear and straightforward, others shrouded in mystery. Sometimes the enormous energy of the man lay dormant, awaiting a spark that would send him on a crusade for bettering the lives of the people from whom he sprang. He dreamed beyond the mountains that surrounded his beloved Margaree. And he came to understand the barriers in the minds of the people with whom he worked, and encouraged them to transcend these barriers. Over the years, he discovered some mountains that he could not cross – in himself and in the forces that controlled the lives of the people he loved. But always, he sought the passes through these barriers with courage and enthusiasm.

"Mighty Moses"

> The climate of Atlantic Canada seems excellent for breeding greatness, but not for nurturing it.
>
> —Alexander Laidlaw, *The Man from Margaree*

As the eldest boy in the family, Coady was "doing a man's work when I was ten." Farm life suited him, and the young lad grew up strong and healthy. Porridge made from homegrown oats ground at the local grist mill, wheat biscuits, gaspereau, salmon and trout filled out Coady's big frame. Stories of his Irish ancestors – their battles, trials and tribulations – filled his imagination.

As Coady grew up, the economy of Cape Breton began to change radically as rural communities lost their people to the booming industrial area around Sydney. Steel mills arose and coal mines expanded. Thousands of people from Europe and the local children of farmers, fishermen and woodsmen moved to the flourishing towns. Sons wanted better opportunities than their fathers, and daughters craved the bright lights of the cities of the Boston States where informal networks ensured them good positions as domestics. As he raked hay and tended the farm animals, Coady must have been familiar with stories of the tearful farewells that marked the exodus of young men and women from his rural utopia. The homeleavers would live among strangers in impersonal cities, far from the supportive kinship system that held communities together.

But perhaps they could stay home and make good lives for themselves if farms could be made more productive and profitable. If Coady was to help this process, he would need a good education. As the eldest son, he could have taken over the family farm. But he had a larger vision for himself, and wanted to go beyond the mountain, learn all he could, and return to revitalize his home community.

Life on the farm "made my early education spotty.... I did not go to school regularly until I was about fifteen years old," Coady recalled. His parents home-schooled their son, who showed a flair for mathematics. Coady, a friend noted, had "the soul of a poet," but he had the mind of a mathematician, and the two strains in his character were ever at odds with each other. Coady's creative imagination constantly soared beyond the mundane and the everyday as he envisaged his ideal society where people could live what he called "the good and abundant life." His mathematical bent led him to seek the blueprint, the formulae, the scientific route to this life.

Coady attended the school at Margaree Forks, finding there "the most inspiring teacher of my life." Chris Tompkins, the principal, another double cousin of Coady's, recognized the potential of this big country lad and did all he could to foster it. At the end of the nineteenth century, teaching offered intelligent young men and women a way to stay in their home province and make a living. The profession, although poorly paid, was respectable. Coady saw his future in it, shaping young minds. He did well in his final exams at the Margaree Forks school, moving to Truro in 1900 to train as a teacher at the Normal School. Teachers there rated the young man's performance as "fair" while considering him "industrious and solid rather than intellectual." Coady received a teaching diploma, and returned to the "very school in which I was taught and inspired." At Margaree Forks, he taught fifteen subjects in three grades for six hours a day, 216 days a year, for $140. He studied Greek and Roman history and Latin in his spare time. "I loved these subjects and laid the foundations for a very successful college career," he explained. In the summers, he worked on the family farm, keeping his feet on the ground and building up his physique through hard work.

In 1903, Coady registered at Saint Francis Xavier University (St. F.X.) to study English, mathematics, church history, philosophy, Latin and Greek. He read a great deal of poetry to feed his imagination, especially Shakespeare, Tennyson, Burns and Kipling. Poems such as Kipling's "If" – "If you can keep your head when all about you/Are losing theirs and blaming it on you…" – inspired him to examine his own potential.

Coady became a college athlete, throwing the hammer, playing on the football team, earning the name "Mighty Moses from Margaree." He also won medals in Greek, philosophy, Latin and history, graduating at the top of his class in 1905 and qualifying for a Grade A teaching certificate.

Then another Tompkins changed the direction of his life. Jimmy Tompkins, with whom he had grown up, was twelve years older than Moses. Jimmy had gone to Rome in 1897 to study for the priesthood. From there he had tutored Coady by correspondence in Latin and Greek. He also dispatched to his cousin "a steady stream of pamphlets and books. They appealed to the boy in me and I walked on thin air…thinking of great things for the future."

The young country boy had grown up, tall and strong. He had done well at university, impressing his fellow students and his teachers. His cousin's letters from Rome excited him, and led to qualms about his future vocation as a teacher.

Coady had travelled beyond the mountain. He recognized that "There were people in that outside world, too, people with difficulties similar to or greater than those known by the early settlers of Margaree. In fact, it was to escape some of these hardships that my ancestors had come to this snug valley."

While on a visit to Reserve Mines, Coady was reading the penny edition of the Gospel of Saint Luke that his cousin had sent him from Rome. He heard the great bell of St.Joseph's calling the faithful to mass. Struck by the continuity of the same message across the centuries from the days of the apostles to the present, the young man decided to become a priest.

And so he went to Rome

A Time in Rome

> This was an unprecedented opportunity for a poor boy from
> the country to see the world…

> —Moses Coady

Although it was but a small university in a remote part of the British Empire, a number of professors at St. F.X. had studied in the United States and Europe, giving the place a cosmopolitan air. The Propaganda College in Rome allocated a place to a student from St. F.X. and Coady was selected to fill it. At the centre of the Catholic world, Coady would "enjoy the inspiration of a five-year sojourn…and get the best in theological and philosophical training of the time." After helping with farm work, Coady left for Rome in October 1905. He loved life in the Eternal City. Rome was transformed in the decades after it became the capital of Italy in 1870. New roads had been driven through old neighbourhoods, gardens lined the Tiber, and ancient ruins and signs of its former imperial grandeur lay all around. All roads still led to Rome, where the Vatican struggled to come to terms with the modern world amid the splendours and symbols of its glorious past. Coady revelled in life here; the poor boy from the country was constantly stimulated by what he saw and heard. He studied Italian, attended the opera and learned arias from *Il Travatore* and *Carmen*. These he would sing years later in his fine baritone voice, back home in his office in Antigonish, the remembered words floating out through the transom and along the hallway. Recalling his time in Rome, Coady wrote to a friend:

I remember how sweet was the sound of the voices of the representatives of so many nations of the earth singing the praise of the Blessed Virgin on the eve of the Immaculate Conception. We were the living proof of the fulfilment of her prophecy: "Behold from henceforth all nations shall be called blessed." I count my sojourn in the Propaganda as the greatest piece of luck in my life.

Coady studied for his doctorate for two years at the Academy of St. Thomas, named for the thirteenth-century Italian scholastic philosopher and theologian. A prolific writer, Thomas Aquinas came to have enormous intellectual authority in the church as he sought to connect Aristotle's thought to Christian doctrines of faith and reconciliation. Thomism became the general teaching of the Catholic Church. The Antigonish Movement would use this theology in a radical way. Coady and the other leaders drew upon the writings of St. Thomas to conjure up images of human beings and the life they could lead. They would contrast them with the grim social realities in eastern Nova Scotia, the indignities imposed upon them by powerful people, and the general misery in which so many people lived. The lot of human beings could be improved, but not under the present system of exploitation that laid such burdens on the poor and the powerless. Catholics should reject this system as immoral, and strive to bring into being a better, more just and wholesome society.

Coady, with his mathematical mind, warmed to Thomism. Society was knowable through the exercise of reason, and its underlying laws could be discovered. Science, rationality, and logical thought, as propounded by St. Thomas, would lead the way to a better life for Catholics. Find the laws of progress, lay them out in clear terms, spread them widely among those struggling to make sense of their lives and to escape from poverty and dependency, and the ideal society would come into being. Coady laid the ideas of Aquinas over his memories of the idyllic days he had spent in the Margaree and came up with what he thought was the template for the good and abundant life for all.

After his immersion in Thomism, Coady spent three more years in study, acquiring another doctorate and preparing for ordination as a Catholic priest. He was ordained in St. John Lateran church by Cardinal Respighi on May 10, 1910.

The qualities that would distinguish the reverend doctor in later life – a charismatic presence, an exciting teaching style, the ability to simplify complex issues and talk about them in vivid language that everyone could understand, and powerful oratory – emerged after he completed his formal education. Coady not only had a logical mind and a poetic imagination, he was also possessed of a certain playfulness and a warm humanity that encouraged him to seek the good in all people.

The newly ordained priest spent the summer of 1910 wandering around Europe. He visited the home territory of his ancestors in Ireland before returning to Canada. A photograph of him taken around this time shows a tall, solemn young man in a long black cassock, a "slim but proud Levite," in his own words. In August, he made a triumphal return to the Margaree to say his first mass. The austere routine and meagre food in the seminary had not dented the spirit or damaged the health of the tough young country lad who had returned lean and fit from the centre of the Catholic world with two doctorates. His parents were particularly joyful at the achievements of their eldest son.

The new priest was brought down to earth by two neighbours. Medric and his wife, Sarah, had passed a trying winter, plagued by illness. Coady sought to console them by reminding the couple that God often visited his people with tribulations. Medric replied, "A visit from the Lord, indeed it was, Father Moses, but why a visit that lasted all winter?" Throughout his life, Coady stayed in touch with the people of his community, counselling and encouraging them – and being challenged by simple questions from simple folk like Medric, questions that kept him grounded in the lives of ordinary people.

In later life, Coady wrote about a problem he had confronted and which other bright young men and women would also have to consider as they looked around at a countryside in decline and tried to decide whether to stay home or seek greener fields beyond their mountains:

> The bright child who gives signs of intelligence in school is immediately picked for a different career from that in which he was born. Rural people will mortgage their farms, and workers will contribute their savings to the last cent, to see that a favoured boy or girl gets a so-called chance in life....
>
> In our present educational procedure – which is essentially a skimming process – we are robbing our rural and industrial population of the natural leaders.

After Coady returned from Rome, the president of St. F.X., Rev. Dr. Hugh MacPherson, asked Bishop John Cameron if Dr. Moses Coady could join his staff. The bishop readily agreed, and the young priest seemed set for a career in academic life. He joined five other new appointees who had studied in Europe and the United States. In 1912, MacPherson expressed his hope for St. F.X.:

> The policy of getting our professors educated in the most celebrated universities of Europe and America will soon have us supplied with men whose standing cannot be discounted and whose names will be an advertisement for us all over the country.

As James Cameron, the historian of the university, would put it nearly a century later, "He clearly had a desire for an improved public image." MacPherson's hopes would be realized, but in a different way from what he envisaged: Coady would develop and pioneer a new approach to education and learning that owed little to the established European and American universities. It would grow from the soil of Nova Scotia. He would become a world leader in adult education and put St. F.X. on the world map as a centre for this way of learning. When Coady took up his position at St. F.X., he was none too pleased with some of his duties. He was assigned to teach Latin and mathematics in the high school attached to the university, and supervise the students in the residential hall on the campus, known as "The Alleys." Coady described himself as a "kind of *facchino*" an Italian word for "porter." However, in later life, he realized this lowly position was preparing him "for the future job of building the economy of Maritime Canada."

Father Jimmy's Crusade

> For us, what the people most need to learn must be what they most want to learn. Let there be the least trace of superiority or propagandism in our attitude, let the people once think of us as academic persons come to force our preconceptions upon them, and the undertaking is dead.
>
> —Father Jimmy Tompkins

Father Jimmy Tompkins, now vice-president of St. F.X., welcomed his cousin to the university. Father Jimmy had begun laying the foundation of what would become the Antigonish Movement, and he saw in Coady an ally in the cause he had begun to espouse. With a few other far-sighted priests on and off the campus, he had seen the need for the university to put its learning resources at the disposal of the ordinary people of the region rather than simply educating future elites. Farmers, fishermen, woodsmen and others were finding it harder and harder to make a decent living as the local economy moved from being based on subsistence to depending on market demand. "Little Doc" Hugh MacPherson, the Dean of Engineering, helped farmers to improve the quality of their products. Father Michael Gillis, a parish priest who had studied at the London School of Economics, pressured the university to serve the people whose donations supported it and the diocese. He urged the government to appoint agricultural representatives (ag. reps.) and promoted the scientific training of farmers and the education of women in home economics. Coady described Gillis as "the creative mind behind all these movements, the dynamic leader and inspirer."

Father Jimmy had joined St. F.X. in 1902 as professor of Greek and higher algebra, as well as college librarian. By the time Coady arrived on the campus, Father Jimmy had begun to have doubts about the direction of university education. His room became the meeting place for the dissidents on campus who shared his concerns. He developed a contempt for many of his colleagues in this small, clerically dominated institution. An acerbic man, he did not conceal his feelings. Father Jimmy saw the coats with long tails, greened with age, that the academics wore as symbolizing their dedication to antiquated ideas about education. Of one man, he said, "You could grow potatoes in his coat tail." Could traditional academics lead the farmers, fishermen and other toilers out of poverty? Father Jimmy doubted it. He recognized that these people had to keep on learning to survive. In later life, he wrote:

> Our experience in the Antigonish Movement is that there is more real Adult Education at the pit heads, down in the mines, out among the fishermen's shacks, along the wharves, and wherever the farmers gather to sit and talk in the evenings, than you can get from one hundred thousand dollars' worth of fossilized formal courses. It springs from the heart and the pains of the people.

Father Jimmy did not want his university simply to give its existing courses in small communities. He sought a radical restructuring of the relationship between teachers and learners:

> Every great teacher the world has ever seen went to the people, not so much to teach or inspire as to learn and to be inspired and encouraged to press on. The inspired teacher and the sympathetic listener mutually reacted upon each other and both became great.

Coady noted that his cousin had "boundless faith in the ordinary man." But Tompkins was critical of some of his fellow clergy: "Many of our young clergymen, as an observant layman remarked, cannot read without exciting the laughter and pity of the average listener."

Like Coady, Father Jimmy deplored the skimming of the youth and potential leaders from the region. But he also saw another, far more dangerous skimming process taking place in the economy of the Maritime Provinces: "The injury done to [the region] by the absence of banking institutions, controlled within the provinces and by our own people, is far-reaching and irreparable." International capitalists looked for possibilities for big and quick returns, anywhere in the world, "thinking little about the fishermen, miners or farmers of Nova Scotia."

Such men would supply firms in Montreal and Toronto with money to open branches in the Maritimes. "And thus control of our industries moves west – so do the profits. Maritimers do the servile work and profit accordingly." Father Jimmy called the monopolists and financial despots "Cream Skimmers."

In 1912, his ideas about the role of the university crystallized after he attended a meeting in London of academic institutions in Britain involved in adult education. Rising literacy and increasing class consciousness in that country had generated a new kind of worker, one who sought to continue his or her education after leaving school and taking jobs. The Workers' Educational Association, founded in 1903, brought together working-class people and teachers in university education departments. Emphasis was placed on lectures, tutorials, and regular reading and writing at home by those interested in long and thorough courses of study.

Father Jimmy returned from London on fire with the idea of turning St. F.X. into a people's university. But even though he was a vice-president of the institution, he found little enthusiasm for his cause among his colleagues.

Father Jimmy's magpie mind collected ideas and experiences for his cause. The British approach towards adult education rested on a belief that learning for learning's sake was the key to enriching the lives of workers. The Antigonish Movement would follow another path, using adult education as a practical way for individuals and communities to lift themselves out of poverty and helplessness. In the United States, adult education fostered self-improvement. The Danish approach strengthened national identity while revitalizing the countryside through folk schools.

Between 1912 and 1922, Father Jimmy hammered out his philosophy of adult education and attracted more people to his crusade. Personal development and self-help would be encouraged and harmonized with efforts to improve communities and enhance the collective good. Individuals, given access to the knowledge they needed to improve their lives, would work with others to revitalize and transform their communities. Father Jimmy also voiced his views on the university, Catholic education and the local power elite – to their detriment. He wrote articles for *The Casket*, the Antigonish community newspaper, and launched the Forward Nova Scotia Movement to stimulate action against rural decline. He claimed this enterprise was "decidedly a movement for the whole community, Protestant and Catholic, irrespective of politics or religion."

The outbreak of the First World War in August 1914 both aided and inhibited Father Jimmy's crusade. Many of the clergy, including Michael Gillis, served with front-line troops, and the men of eastern Nova Scotia joined the army by the thousands. From Cape Breton alone, 13,000 people went to war. Moses Coady thought of becoming an army padre, and phoned his bishop to determine his response. The bishop told the young priest about a dream he'd had. Coady had become a padre, and sailed on a troopship to Europe. It had been sunk and he had been lost. Moses Coady decided to stay at the university, but his ideas about his work in adult education began to be expressed in military language, influenced by his discussions with Michael Gillis and Fathers Archibald MacDonald and Miles Tompkins, another cousin who had been to war. Coady spoke of his work as "an intellectual bombing operation."

The First World War used the latest technology to kill large numbers of soldiers and civilians. This conflict marked a watershed in world history. No longer could ordinary people trust their leaders to look after their interests or to care for them. Everyone had to develop a critical consciousness about the world and their place in it. It was necessary to encourage what Father Jimmy called "educative democracy." People had to think globally and act locally. To do this effectively, they needed to keep learning how to act together to create better lives for themselves. As Tompkins put it,

> Men and women everywhere are clamouring for the equal opportunity that education and intellectual training [offer]....
> There have not been two types of V.C.s [Victoria Crosses] nor two types of wooden crosses in the Flanders Field.

Ordinary people had served and suffered during the war "and now that peace has come they seek an equal share of opportunities and in the good and worthwhile things in life." During the war, "educational extension" – which later became known as adult education – had made a beginning in efforts to inform soldiers and others what the conflict was all about. In 1917, the Canadian YMCA and the chaplain service of the Canadian Army set up Khaki College, where 50,000 learners studied to prepare themselves for the post-war world. The college was directed by Dr. Henry Marshall Tory, president of the University of Alberta, which had pioneered the process of taking knowledge to people where they lived and worked.

While his cousin promoted the cause of adult education and upset more and more people on and off the St. F.X. campus while attracting very few followers, Coady became an effective teacher, enthusiastic, compassionate and persuasive. Coady took a particular interest in teacher education, seeing it as the key to the creation of the kind of society he envisaged for the region. He took a special interest in all his students. Many graduates recalled later the influence Coady had upon them: "I never would have made it, had it not been for the grounding in the matriculation subjects and the 'Mosaic Law' that made it stick," one said.

Justice Keiller MacKay studied Latin with Coady, and wrote to him years later:

> I still remember and once again acknowledge with gratitude
> your real contribution to the development of my education,
> and especially for instilling in my youthful mind an urge and
> love for the classics. Your part in stimulating an appreciation
> of the beautiful in literature and poetry in the minds of all your
> students has been large and of great profit.

While teaching those destined for professional careers, Coady must have had his doubts. Would these people help to bring into being a new society, or simply pursue their own individual interests? He earned the gratitude and affection of many future leaders who would support him when he became director of the Extension Department.

Coady gained a reputation as "the saver of hopeless causes" and put on special classes for students who might otherwise have failed. In his second year, some of them gave him a calabash pipe and an address of appreciation. (Coady smoked the pipe for a while, but gave it up in favour of cigars.) He prided himself in the belief that he could teach anyone mathematics. With abundant energy, he was a tireless worker. But he had an impatient edge, and could be a hard taskmaster.

A woman who attended a summer course given by Coady recalled how crowded the lecture became with students, some of whom had not registered for the course. They sat on the floor and on the windowsills to hear this inspiring speaker. Coady was honing the oratorical skills, dynamic presentation style and the ability to convey complex concepts in simple ways to learners that would stand him in good stead when he moved into adult education. But he had little patience with those he considered laggards. When a pre-med student could make no sense of a long equation that Coady scrawled on the blackboard, Coady held the man up to ridicule: "You'll never make a good medical doctor – I can tell by the way you go at a problem in algebra. You'll be taking a man's appendix out when the trouble is in his gall bladder." The student whom Coady lambasted became a successful surgeon.

The dynamic teacher impressed the university hierarchy, and they sent him to the Catholic University in Washington, DC, to take a master's degree in education in 1914. Here he could learn all about the "psychological and philosophical aspects of education, as well as its historical development." St. F.X. had the bright young man in mind as head of a proposed School of Education. While in Washington, Coady heard from his cousin Father Jimmy with advice about learning to speak well. Tompkins stressed the need to move from abstract discussions about education; he wanted Coady to see how he could make a difference in the world outside academia.

When he returned to Antigonish, Coady was appointed principal of St. F.X.'s University High School and began to teach summer schools for teachers in Halifax. He had decided that his "destiny was to work with teachers and help to regenerate the country through the education of the youth." The priest also attended diocesan meetings and witnessed how rural and urban society were changing and his people sliding into poverty and despair.

2

The Sorcerer's Apprentice: Tompkins and Coady

Here I am with two doctoral degrees from Rome and a Master's degree from Washington. Surely to God, I should be able to do something positive and progressive for the farm people of this county.

—Moses Coady

In 1920, Coady attended a Farmers' Exhibition or Fall Fair with his cousin Father Miles Tompkins. This priest managed Mount Cameron, the university farm, and had been a padre during the Great War. After the war, he visited Denmark, being greatly impressed with the agricultural development of that country. The two men must have been dismayed at the poor quality of the produce they saw at the fair. Tompkins told Coady about the high standards of Danish products and the success that the Danes had in exporting them.

Coady and Tompkins organized the first People's School on the campus of St. Francis Xavier University in 1921. A photo shows them sitting with the soberly clad participants. Father Jimmy looks straight at the camera while Coady lifts his eyes heavenwards. In reflecting on this event, Coady noted: "It was nothing less than a revelation to observe what an amount of latent intellectual talent has been lying around undeveloped, and thereby precluded from attaining its proper destiny both as to individual needs and for the country's best welfare."

His approach to adult education owed much to his cousin. A friend said of Father Jimmy,

> He was forever urging people to read and study and activate their minds.... He believed implicitly in the power of people to accomplish anything if they would but awaken to the opportunities of the moment and use their collective energies in a determined effort to improve their status.

Also in 1921, Father Jimmy published *Knowledge for the People*, an appeal to his university to implement a program of adult education. While Coady was in Washington, his cousin's letters told him how wonderfully well things were going with his crusade. It seemed the time was ripe for the priest's ideas to be put into action. Gifted young men and women were leaving the region to find their fortune elsewhere. As Dawn Fraser wrote in *Echoes from Labour's Wars* in 1925, "The winter winds are bleak and drear/I'd better move from here." In the 1920s, the Maritimes lost 150,000 people and the countryside began to look somewhat empty.

In *Knowledge for the People*, Father Jimmy came up with an interesting but unrealistic idea. A group of dedicated adult educators would travel the highways and byways of the region, offering advice and direction to anyone who would listen to them. These people would be volunteers, and find ready acceptance because, as Father Jimmy put it, Nova Scotia "was pregnant with sympathy for improvement of the education system."

Father Jimmy kept up his crusade, but in 1922 was ejected from St. F.X. and sent as parish priest to Canso. Before he went into exile, Father Jimmy had called for accountability by the university, pointing out that such institutions are "living organisms whose roots are in the people, and unless they draw from these roots, the material of life, the tree will die, will be cut down and burnt."

When he realized that he would lose his university position – and the power that went with it – and simply become another parish priest, Father Jimmy sought Coady's advice. "What if I go away from here entirely?" he asked. "They're looking for priests." Coady replied, "Go to Canso. Go and obey your bishop. Go!" This encounter illustrates the differences between the two men and marks a turning point in the history of the Antigonish Movement. Coady's mentor had now turned to him for advice, and Coady's response typified his approach.

When the energetic, innovative Tompkins was rusticated for supporting university amalgamation in the Maritimes, his cousin and two other priests travelled with him to Mulgrave to see him embark on the steamer for Canso. The contrast between the two men was in more than their physical appearance. Coady stood over two metres (6 feet) tall and weighed around 100 kilos (220 pounds) in his prime. His cousin stood just over one and a half metres tall and weighed about 50 kilos. White faced, with white hands, Father Jimmy looked frail. Sharp-featured, he had a nose like a knife blade and a firm jaw. His large blue eyes pierced the hearts of those he met. But his voice was querulous and squeaky. Well aware of his unprepossessing appearance, he knew he did not have the temperament or stamina to lead the social movement he envisioned. He was too much of a loner, too abrasive, too scornful of the frailties of others.

Coady, with his mathematical bent, thought in straight lines, ever seeking certainty of the sort that marked this field, where two and two always made four. Father Jimmy, a man of twists and turns, had a non-linear mind, constantly shooting off in all directions. To him, two and two could just as easily add up to 22. Coady, in modern terminology, operated inside the box, Father Jimmy outside it.

Father Jimmy was suspicious of boxes. He had seen how large, authoritarian, hierarchical, paternalistic institutions like his university and his church reacted to change by digging in their heels and smothering dissent. He became a kind of shaman, operating on the margin between order and chaos, the campus and the community, seeking to break universities out of their accustomed ways and people out of their inertia. In Canso, he would continue to work the magic that would start a great social movement and transform hundreds of communities.

Coady wrote of his cousin that he was "of a kind that defies classification by ordinary rules…. He was a personality of many facets…. He could be illogical when an idea dominated him." Coady's prescriptive style contrasted with the way in which his cousin offered advice. Tompkins would say, "Here's a book [or a pamphlet, or a press clipping, or an article] on your problem. Read it and make up your own mind about what you are going to do." As a friend put it, "Father Jimmy wouldn't even put out the cat for you. But he'd stay up half the night nagging you to do it."

Coady, at home in the classroom and on public platforms, could not "talk privately for five minutes without teaching," claimed Ned Corbett, another pioneer adult educator. Tompkins, according to a visitor, was "a great little man, a genius, full of ideas.... He couldn't teach a class, though, he gets so many ideas and jumps around from thing to thing: he's always going round and round."

Joseph Hernon, who knew both men, called them "humble giants" and wrote about the differences between them in an article in the February 1960 issue of *Atlantic Advocate*:

> [Father Jimmy] was no Coady. He worked best in his glebe house with a small group in whom he had cannily spotted the potential for leadership.
>
> There is no question that Tompkins visualized Coady as the heart and voice of any real movement that might emerge from his thinking.... When they were youngsters, Coady gave him the physical support the older boy needed. And Tompkins kindled the flames of learning and social thought in the brash young giant. He counselled him through youth and during studies in Rome. He saw in Coady the commanding personality he could never have and he set about to groom him for the future he envisioned.

The approaches of the two men to adult education differed, but they were united in seeing the process as a way of encouraging local democracy and decision-making. Alex Laidlaw pointed out that Coady "was a fervent democrat.... For him, the world had had enough of rule by a few strong men at the top. A new age would dawn, he believed, when the whole mass of humanity would lift itself to a new level of life, when democratic man would emerge."

With Father Jimmy, the leader and main proponent of adult education at the university, in the wilderness, it looked as if the movement he had launched would run out of steam. But he had created a critical mass of believers, and they continued to pressure St. F.X. to do something to revitalize the countryside and to help people to make better lives for themselves and to work together for the good of others.

Coady, Tompkins and others – such as Father Michael Gillis, who played a prominent role in this initiative – changed the image of the priest in Eastern Nova Scotia. As Joe Laben, a coal miner and co-operative organizer put it,

> Prior to Father Jimmy, we were scared of priests. We had some very cross priests that would never bother with people at all. They would give them hell and brimstone and the devil and a

lot of superstitious stuff. We were so inferior and afraid. They preached fear of God rather than love of God.

Organizing the Teachers

The widespread apathy towards public education in Nova Scotia chills like an east wind.

—*Education in the Maritime Provinces of Canada,*
Carnegie Foundation Report (1922)

In Coady's time, teachers in Atlantic Canada faced an uphill struggle. A boy was expected to leave school as soon as possible to help on the family farm or work with his father in the small boat fishery. Daughters in large families left school to look after their siblings and do farm work, or went to work in the Boston States, sending money home to help the family.

Public education in Nova Scotia, according to the Carnegie report, had become a political football. The province paid less per pupil in government support than any other jurisdiction in Canada, save Prince Edward Island. Teachers lacked qualifications, and about half of them earned less than $430 a year. Bullied by trustees and parents, teachers tried several times to organize themselves to improve their salaries and working conditions. The United Teachers' Association of Nova Scotia was founded in May 1862 to encourage "the elevation of the professional and social status of the teacher." In 1895, teachers in the province formed a new union, but continued to work against each other, offering to work for less money than their colleagues. They also suffered the impositions of what one teacher called "some trustees and the unrighteous magistrate who prefers to purchase the favour of his neighbours by unjustly condemning the unprotected teacher."

W.T. Kennedy, principal of the Halifax Academy, pointed out in 1921 what needed to be done to better the lot of teachers:

Teachers taken singly are a rope of sand, weak and easily demolished: but teachers united in a single body, such as this Union proposed, would present a very different face to any attempt at oppression or persecution.... Let us strive to develop an esprit de corps that will prevent teachers from any attempt to displace and underbid each other.

Kennedy noted the example of a woman in a remote area who made life miserable for every teacher who came to the school.

It had become a perfect mania with that woman to keep the teacher in hot water. One teacher joined the union, and sent the letters he received from the woman to the secretary. The council told her that it was awaiting orders to take action against her for conspiracy. Not a teacher in that section has ever been molested since.

Efforts to make the union effective were futile. The emphasis in the early part of the 20th century was on raising salaries. One of the union leaders advised, "We live in an age of combines. Teachers should unite, form a Bureau and pledge themselves not to take less than the minimum salary acknowledged proper for the section." The problems in the union stemmed from apathy. Four-fifths of teachers were women in a macho society; when they married, they lost their jobs. Government officials dominated the union. Although they tried to be helpful, their efforts aroused resentment among the rank and file. In 1920, the teachers excluded government officials from union meetings, believing that they "should formulate their policies and conduct their affairs without official interference."

A chance remark by a visitor led Coady to get involved. The teachers' union faced two choices – disband or revitalize itself. Coady was invited to attend a meeting in Truro at Easter 1921 when these options would be discussed. He had no great enthusiasm for the organization, telling a friend that he was not particularly interested in a body called a "Union." The word had bad connotations in many quarters. However, on the day Coady was to take the night train to Truro, he met Dr. William Learned of the Carnegie Corporation for the Advancement of Teaching, who was studying the state of public education in the Maritimes. Coady recalled the encounter:

> When I told him that I was to attend the meeting of the teachers' union, he voiced his opinion that the organization of teachers was our white hope. I went to the meeting determined to protest the disbanding of the teachers' union, however weak and inefficient it was.

Coady loved challenges and hopeless causes, but he was not prepared for what happened when he arrived in Truro to support the union. The other six people at the meeting asked him what alternatives he could offer to disbandment. He had a ready answer: hire a paid organizer who would also edit the union publication. Those at the meeting decided he was the man for the job: "I was stunned when they unanimously asked me to take on these tasks," he later said. Coady became the union's secretary-treasurer, and founded and edited the *Nova Scotia Teachers' Bulletin*. He put his logical mind to work, and came up with a set of proposals that teachers and the people of Nova Scotia should demand: better schools, a minimum salary for teachers, schools of education at universities and the involvement of universities in the school system to promote public education, an Education Week in the province to increase public awareness, and the selection of female trustees in rural schools.

Coady went on the road "with great seriousness" to meet with teachers and press the case for organizing them. He began in eastern Nova Scotia, "where such an idea had not received any consideration." The publication of the Carnegie report in 1922 aided his cause.

As always, the priest looked beyond the mountains surrounding the teachers. His vision of the future of the union transcended their narrow interests. The task of this body had to be "not a mere cry for higher salaries, or a threat to strike, but a spirit of duty to give the people of the country the best possible service." Although the province-wide union appeared to be falling apart before Coady took it over, strong locals with dedicated leaders operated in Halifax, Amherst, Truro and New Glasgow.

Coady helped to draft a series of resolutions addressed to Premier E.H. Armstrong and Dr. Henry Munro, superintendent of education. They suggested that the county be the unit of taxation and administration for education, the course of study for teachers be revised and minimum qualifications for them be set, and Education Week be officially declared.

The government issued permissive licenses to people with no professional training in education to enable them to teach. The union wanted these licenses abolished. Coady accompanied a union delegation to a meeting with the provincial cabinet, which received a "very cordial and sympathetic response." The issues of salaries, licenses, pensions and grants were discussed and the delegation "left believing that every effort would be made to bring about desired changes."

But the government did nothing, and on June 3, 1922, the union censured it.

The teachers, and the press, soon began to see Coady as a clear speaker and a keen thinker with a fine command of language. He had the ability to cut through the fog surrounding the system, expose its shortcomings and suggest ways to overcome them. In the *Teachers' Bulletin* for December 1922, Coady pinpointed a problem that would obsess him in the years to come – the waste of human potential in the region. Bright and able men and women went into the mines, the woods, office work or domestic service because "teaching offers them nothing." The article lamented "a weird pessimism [that] so benumbed everybody that nothing has been attempted to break the spell." Coady's organizing efforts with the union basically aimed to better the lot of teachers. But the priest had a broader vision: to reverse the growing gloom in the province as more and more young people left and the economy changed for the worse.

He broke through personal apathy and institutional inertia by working with teachers at the local level. Notices went out to all teachers. They established executives in communities. The local leaders signed up other teachers, collected union dues, kept half for themselves, and remitted the balance to Coady. By February 1923, almost half the teachers in Nova Scotia had joined the union. Coady expected his logical approach to be adopted without question, and found it "rather humiliating" when he had to argue the case for a strong union. In doing so, he refined his powers of persuasion. In the *Bulletin*, he pointed out the need to appeal to the self-interest of parents. Many who sent their children to boarding schools would support local schools if they were improved. Coady also pressed the case for having more women on school boards.

In 1924, the government cut teachers' salaries. That same year, St. F.X. established a Department of Education and appointed Coady to head it. He resigned his post with the union to return to academic life. While organizing the teachers, he had already begun to have doubts about his original idea of changing society by improving the education of the young: "Our greatest hope for progress is in further education for grown-ups," he wrote. "There are many means for doing this, by extension courses, by the press, by the platform lecture and every aid in this respect should be used to the utmost."

Organizing the teachers and championing their cause had provided him with another kind of apprenticeship. In just over three years, he had saved a failing organization and breathed new life into the membership with his optimistic and positive attitude. In eastern Nova Scotia and elsewhere, Coady made friends and contacts who would be helpful to him when he took up the cause of adult education; principals would open their schools for him in the evenings for community meetings. Coady also recognized that the government could not be relied upon for support as people tried to improve their status and efficiency. Embattled groups had to rely on self-help, mutual aid and strong organizational efforts if they were to improve their lot. The union, after he left, relied on teachers, not government officials, to run it. Civil servants could be helpful, but they had to be "on tap, not on top," if they were to avoid killing the revitalized body with kindness. In unity lay strength, he told them. The teachers had to improve themselves, become more proficient in their profession, keep in touch with modern trends in education and see beyond their narrow interests to work for the good of the community.

Beginnings in Adult Education

> The time is ripe for a vigorous program of adult education in this country.
>
> —Moses Coady, *The People's School: Its Purpose, Its History, What Professors, Students and the Public Say About It* (1922)

With Father Jimmy in exile in Canso, the cause of adult education in eastern Nova Scotia needed a champion. Although his cousin had singled him out for this role, Coady was not sure he was the right person for the task. He spoke vaguely about the need for taking knowledge to the people, but after leaving the teachers' union, he recalled:

> [I] was still dreaming of regenerating the country through the teachers and the education of the youth. Going to the people, in my thinking, was an indirect action and would have to wait for the next generation. I held this view, notwithstanding the fact that a lot of work has been done by St. F.X. professors to carry knowledge to the people.

The province had appointed Hugh "Little Doc" MacPherson as its first agricultural representative (ag. rep.) in 1914. The People's Schools in which Coady had participated had opened his eyes to the great enthusiasm shown by adult learners, but he was realistic enough to know that his university would not leap into the field of adult education as Father Jimmy had expected it to do. Knowledge for the People had summarized his cousin's ideas and come up with a completely unrealistic idea for promoting the cause of adult education through disciples who would not be paid to spread the word about it.

Sometime after leaving the union, Coady had what he called a "brainstorm":

> I would go to my native Margaree and there build a new type of school that would bring music and art to the people of that highly artistic and beautiful country. Perhaps some great musi-

cians and artists, I thought, might come out of such country, so calculated to lift the human heart.

Coady's poetic soul emerged in this scheme to help his people. In 1923, he sent a petition from Catholic and Protestant leaders in the Margaree and Chéticamp to the Sisters of Saint Martha, an order that had come into being to serve the priests and the students at St. F.X. Coady saw their potential for moving beyond these tasks. His petition asked them to take over the public school, set up a domestic science boarding institute, and staff a small hospital. It sought assurance that this work would be done in two or three years, concluding, "We feel that the Sisters of Saint Martha would be able to do this combined educational and health work in a manner most satisfactory to all concerned." Coady had seen the population of his home community, Southwest Margaree, lose 200 of its population of 1,000 between 1901 and 1921. A modern school staffed by dedicated nuns would surely reverse this trend.

But the nuns did not want to move into rural education. Sister John Baptist Cameron, one of the order's councillors, remarked on Coady's powers of persuasion: "[He] had an answer for every objection. He saw many possibilities in the teaching field, and had the faculty of presenting them very forcibly." He had lots of ideas for fundraising and for new vocations for the congregation. And he had cannily secured the support of Bishop Morrison for his venture.

With the agreement of the sisters, Coady began to organize subscriptions and volunteer labour in the Margaree. One nun reported that he "organized picnics, worked like a Trojan himself in overalls and shirt sleeves until the perspiration rolled off him." He bought a nearby residence as a convent and paid for its fuel supply for the first seven years. The school at Margaree Forks opened in September 1926.

Later in life, Coady recognized that economic development had to precede cultural enrichment in small communities: "Through credit unions, co-operative stores, lobster factories and sawmills, we are laying the foundation for an appreciation of Shakespeare and grand opera."

By the time the school opened, Coady had concluded that change would not come through the traditional system because of "the slow process of elementary and secondary education – formal education in the schools is not enough and never was." While working on the school, Coady was struck by "a bolt from the blue ... an idea that turned out to be the turning point in my life ... my second great opportunity in life." He picked up Father Jimmy's cause and became hooked on adult education. As the drift from the countryside continued, Coady sought the "short, quick, scientific way to progress in the world...through the enlightenment and education of adults."

In mid-July 1924, he called together a dozen of his friends in the Margaree to seek their advice on what should be done. He gave a short speech, asking, "What should people do to get life in this community, and what should they think about and study to enable them to get it?" Then he sat down and listened to his friends' response. By the Christmas vacation, he had held 20 meetings, and "here emerged the technique of adult education known as the Antigonish Movement ... the small study club, issuing in economic group action."

Earlier co-ops in Nova Scotia had been formed in waves. In 1884, Robert Burnett, a clergyman, spoke to fruit growers in the Annapolis Valley in words that Coady would echo: "Middlemen thrive by want of co-operation. They live by the solitary efforts of individual producers." Co-operative creameries were established in 1894, and by 1906 half a dozen fruit growers' co-operatives were operating in the Annapolis Valley. In 1912, an umbrella co-operative enterprise, the United Fruit Company of Nova Scotia, brought together the community ventures. But it had problems; the tensions between the desire of growers for independence and the goal of collective action affected the way managers dealt with co-op members. In 1916, the Maritime United Farmers' Co-operative, chartered in New Brunswick, had branches in Antigonish, Truro, Tatamagouche, Amherst, Springhill and Windsor. In 1921, this network collapsed; only the Antigonish branch survived.

British miners imported co-ops based on the principles established in 1844 by the Rochdale Society of Equitable Pioneers. This group of weavers in that British city, tired of poor-quality goods and being shortchanged by merchants, set up their own collective venture. Based on the ideas of one member/one vote, no discrimination, open membership, cash trading, limited interest on capital, payment of dividends based on volume of business and continuous education, it became the model for all successful co-ops. Miners in Stellarton set up their own venture in 1861. Miners in Cape Breton established the British Canadian Cooperative Society in Sydney Mines in 1906; it became the largest consumer-owned society in North America. Coady paid tribute to this venture: "[It] gave us college people the vision of the possibilities of the common folk and the courage to go against the snobbery of the intellectual elite of the country." Many of the co-ops in the province did not last, even though the government passed legislation to assist their formation. They failed because of poor management, domination by a few individuals, and a lack of ongoing education. Prior to Coady, the individual co-operatives in Nova Scotia did not operate as part of a network headed by a charismatic leader with a vision of how they could lead people to a new world.

Writing 30 years after the first community meetings in the Margaree, Coady recalled his vision of what they could do:

> The formation of these little clubs with others would enroll the whole community. The union of communities gave district action and it could be extended to include the whole country, and the whole world ... that is the very dream that dawned on us as the St. F.X. Extension got under way, and the progress of the movement today bids fair to achieve this result.

Coady's movement would be grown from the grassroots, not suddenly brought into being by immigrants. Such movements require three things for their success: an appeal to the self-interest of participants, a new set of values opposed to those dominating society, and deeply felt convictions.

While Coady went about building the school in the Margaree and thinking through ways to revitalize a land that was losing its best and brightest young people, other forces emerged to forward the cause of adult education. Father Michael Gillis spearheaded the Scottish Catholic Society's efforts to push St. F.X. into that field. The members told the university authorities that if they did not start an adult education program, the society would jump into the field and do so. The St. F.X. Alumni Society also demanded that the university take knowledge to the people. The Rural Conference in 1924 passed a resolution calling for the establishment of an extension program at St. F.X. That year, Father Jimmy attended a meeting organized by Carnegie Corporation on adult education. In Canso, the priest had put arms and legs on his ideas about how people could learn their way out of poverty and despair. He had helped local fishermen build their own lobster factory. But he recognized that something more than local action was needed to resolve the increasing problems in the fisheries as the big trawlers in the offshore dumped their catches on the market, forcing down the prices the inshore fishermen received for theirs. In 1923, he called for a study of the fisheries and continued to petition the federal government on this issue.

Social movements are triggered from agitation to action by certain events that focus discontent and create awareness of a problem. On July 1, 1927, the fishermen expressed their lack of enthusiasm for the 60th anniversary of Canadian confederation by milling around the dock at Canso and bewailing their plight. Urged on by Father Jimmy, they held a mass meeting to discuss their discontents and determine what could be done about them. As Coady put it, "The theme of the meeting was the ancient question heard in Rome in the days of Julius Caesar: 'Wherefore rejoice?' What had confederation done for them? they asked." Father Jimmy ensured that the meeting received sympathetic press coverage and then arranged for a meeting of 40 priests at their annual retreat in Antigonish to pass a resolution urging the provincial and federal governments to assist the fishermen and undertake a study of their industry. Telegrams went out to officials in Ottawa and Halifax, backing up this demand.

Like John the Baptist, Father Jimmy had gone into the wilderness and there prepared the way for his charismatic cousin. From this time onward, his career followed a very different path from Coady's. Father Jimmy remained suspicious of attempts to institutionalize the movement he had brought into being: "When a thing becomes over-institutional-ized, it tends to become sterile."

The federal government reacted to the crisis in the East Coast fisheries by setting up the Royal Commission on the Fisheries of the Maritime Provinces and the Magdalen Islands (the MacLean Commission) in the fall of 1927. The members travelled around the region, visiting small fishing harbours, where they saw idle boats and idle men. In November, they held meetings in Halifax to hear witnesses. The first of these was Moses Coady, who impressed the commission members with his passionate speech and his broad, visionary ideas on what had to be done to save the fisheries – and the region. Maritimers would have to appreciate their resources and think critically. Through a planned economy, small industries could be set up in small communities to provide employment and diversify local economies. Coady cited creameries in the province as evidence of the effectiveness of co-operatives. Most of all, adult education was needed, starting with group and short courses for the fishermen. The 45-year-old priest hammered away at a familiar theme:

> There seems to me to be a philosophy of grand isolation among the universities in the country. They hand pick the country and do nothing for the other classes. Our universities have taken the best brains in the country and exported them. If this Commission would declare a closed season on brains I think it would assist materially.

The MacLean Commission reported in May 1928, presenting a grim document on the state of the fisheries in the region. Fishermen and their families were going hungry and had lost all hope of bettering their situation. The coal fields in Cape Breton had become battlefields between owners and workers.

In November 1928, bowing to pressures from all sides, St. F.X. finally set up a University Extension Department and asked Coady to head it. After hiring A.B. MacDonald as his assistant director, they set off on a six-month tour of eastern and western Canada and the United States to examine what was being done in adult education.

The work of the University of Alberta and the University of Saskatchewan particularly impressed them. Like the provinces, both universities had been founded in 1905. Their presidents recognized that the success of each institution lay in ensuring that they served the needs of the people of the province. The University of Alberta sent its professors into the countryside and emphasized cultural development. Drama, for example, helped to strengthen communities through collective creativity. The University of Saskatchewan focused on ways to improve agriculture in its extension work. Dr. Walter Murray, its president, saw his university engaging in scientific research and disseminating the results to farmers to help them solve their everyday problems.

Coady and A.B. MacDonald returned to Antigonish with their heads full of ideas about adult education, but only the vaguest notions about how to implement them in eastern Nova Scotia. They talked with others about these ideas through the summer of 1929. Where would the money and the teachers come from for this new university initiative? In 1928, the Scottish Catholic Society had suggested that $100,000 be raised for a five-year program of rural education. This move reflected the increasing desperation felt in the region, and was also a squeeze-play to put pressure on St. F.X. to show leadership by setting up a Department of Extension. When the university acted, the Society halted its own efforts and allocated funds to Coady's venture. But before he could move into action, the priest was asked by the P.J.A. Cardin, the federal Minister of Fisheries, to organize the fishermen of the Maritimes. Coady readily agreed and another phase of his career began.

The Fisherman's Friend

My trying ten months—Moses Coady

The general belief was that "only Dr. Coady could do it": bring some cohesion and organization to the fishing industry of the Maritimes. Two others laid claim to the job: Father Albert Boudreau, a priest who had long lamented the plight of the fishermen and M.A. Nickerson, who had organized fishermen on Cape Breton and in Canso. Neither of these men had Coady's physical presence or network of priests and teachers bent on bringing about social and economic change. Coady had a base at St. F.X. His appointment would ensure continuity for attempts to better the lives of fishermen. The fish barons who controlled the marketing of the catches had no objections to the creation of fraternal associations through which fishermen could discuss their common problems, buy supplies and co-operate in acquiring larger boats. But the merchants in the region – middlemen between the big companies and the individual fishermen – feared that such associations would take over the curing and the marketing of fish and act "irresponsibly." Fisheries officers were doing what they could to help the fishermen, but they also had to regulate them and ensure that they did not break the law. So they had a very ambiguous role. An Ottawa insider damned Coady with faint praise, claiming he would be unable to impress the average fisherman: "[Coady] might even lead to awkward and embarrassing situations in the event of questions being asked, as they no doubt will be at the meetings, and end in the Department being ridiculed, at least amongst the non-Catholic fishermen."

Throughout his career, Coady went to great pains to ensure that his efforts to improve the lot of the poor and marginalized people of the region were non-denominational and politically non-partisan.

He set about his organizational work with his usual energy and enthusiasm. But he faced a demanding task.

The inshore fishermen, a highly individualistic group of men, had become sharecroppers of the sea. Securing supplies from local merchants, they went out into the rough Atlantic in small boats. When they returned, the merchants took their fish and deducted its value from what the catchers owed. Some fishermen dried their catches, in the open, and in unhygienic ways; few fishermen paid much attention to the quality of the catch. Nor did they explore ways of marketing it other than the traditional one. The barter system ensured that few people who caught the fish saw any cash. And cash was essential to upgrading their boats and gear and running a more efficient operation. The barter system, although it exploited fishermen and their families, did offer a degree of security, however. The merchants had no interest in losing those whose hard work supported them, and would carry fishermen through bad years and tough times. Often portrayed as the villains of the fishing industry, the merchants were caught in the larger economic system and had little room to change their ways. The lack of what Coady would call "a scientific attitude" frustrated his work with the fishermen throughout the years of the movement. Between 1885 and 1918, the lobster catch in the region dropped from 100 million pounds to 27 million, in part due to the practice of harvesting female lobsters. Fishermen treated the sea like an inexhaustible bank, taking out what they could when they could and never worrying about the future. Changing this lifestyle and the culture associated with it would be no easy task.

Coady began his work with a vision of a better world for all, not just the poor fishermen. He did not believe the problems of the fishing industry could be solved by fiddling around with the existing structures. A new approach was needed, radically different from what had gone before, put into place by those who shared Coady's vision and belief in the ability of ordinary people to master their own destinies. The fishermen need no longer be victims or bystanders: they could become participants if they organized themselves, worked together and formed co-operatives for processing and selling their catches.

As with the teachers, Coady discovered the skeleton of an organization among the fishermen and some good local leaders. He put flesh on the old bones of self-help ventures, and sent new blood coursing through the fishermen's veins with his enthusiasm, energy and commitment to their welfare. In September 1929, Coady spoke to 600 people in the Ideal Theatre in Canso, bringing them hope. He correctly defined their problem: "They weren't looking for handouts ... all they asked for that day was a plan of action." Father Jimmy had nagged at these people for years and helped them to start their own business ventures. Now the local fishermen needed a different type of leadership from someone who could set their needs into a wider context and suggest how to meet them. Field workers in the fisheries welcomed Coady and helped to organize meetings for him to address. He hammered away at one theme: if fishermen wanted to improve their lot, they could do so. As individuals, they had no power. Together, they could learn their way out of their plight by organizing their own co-operatives, studying their situation and finding ways to improve their operations. This powerfully persuasive man did not doubt they could do this.

Word began to spread of this new presence in an industry whose members had lost hope. A new spirit spread in the region as Coady travelled its highways and byways, driving into the smallest fishing communities in his big Buick. A legendary aura began to surround the priest as he pushed himself hard to meet as many people as possible, to inspire them and start them on the road to self-reliance.

One time, near Ship Harbour, east of Halifax, the Buick's brakes froze, and it went into a brook. The jack broke as Coady, knee deep in water, tried to move the heavy car back onto the road. Then he tried to lift the Buick out of the stream by sheer muscle power. That did not work, so he walked three and a half kilometres to Ship Harbour to secure help from the owner of two horses. They failed to move the big car. After changing his socks and eating a good supper, Coady contacted a local garageman, whose tow truck lifted the Buick out of the brook. Coady then headed for Musquodoboit Harbour, arriving at 1:30 in the morning. He found no room at the inn, or anywhere else. So he knocked on the door of A.C. Day, the local fisheries officer, identified himself as "the guy who is organizing the fishermen" and received a warm welcome. Ever the teacher, he spoke to Day's family about social justice for the fishermen and then went to bed.

The December weather in New Brunswick defeated the Buick, so Coady hired a horse and sleigh to travel to the communities. The horse persisted in lying down in front of snowdrifts. The driver dismounted, broke trail, and Coady hauled the sledge through the drifts with the horse following smugly behind him. As well as braving the winter in the Maritimes in 1929–30, Coady visited New York and Boston to examine the impact of steam trawlers on the Atlantic fisheries. They were becoming a persistent concern for the small-boat, inshore fishery because they could deliver large quantities of fish to the markets.

Coady returned to the Margaree for Christmas to relax, and then set out, refreshed, on his crusade. Some communities, like Port Bickerton, welcomed the priest as a saviour. Lunenburg, where the Protestant ethic flourished, saw him as a menace and proved hostile to his message about the need for co-operation in the fisheries.

By the spring of 1930, towards the end of ten trying months, Coady had a clear idea about the way ahead for the fisheries: "When the fishermen of our province get together, and put the best brains of the industry on the problems confronting them we shall get results."

He drafted a constitution for the organization. The United Maritime Fishermen (UMF) would be a co-operative with a strong adult education component.

Coady's commitment to the fishermen's cause was obvious. He piloted his Buick over roads thick with mud in the summer, slippery with ice and blocked by snow in winter. He appeared to be an unstoppable force as he contended with parochial jealousies, ancient ways of fishing, and those who had a vested interest in the established way of carrying on business in the fisheries. This big-hearted man saw latent abilities in every human and sought to harness them to the common good. In his view, if only individuals could see beyond their narrow and immediate problems, look beyond the mountains around them, and work together, there was nothing they could not achieve. He had the knack of turning skeptics into believers by his enthusiasm. Everyone knew he was without personal ambition and did not seek office in the organization he helped to create. Coady realized that the fisheries already had some good leaders. They needed the vision he could give them.

Chester McCarthy, president of the Fisherman's Union of Prince Edward Island, saw Coady's work as simply creating "a sort of fraternal society." He soon changed his mind, however, and attended the founding convention of the UMF in the Masonic Hall in Halifax on June 25 and 26, 1930: McCarthy was elected president of the new organization.

Coady addressed the assembly's 208 delegates. Co-operatives were not simply a device for improving the lives of people in the fisheries, their introduction was "imperatively demanded by the best interests of our civilization." He presented the draft constitution he had prepared, and then left the delegates to organize the new body. This was typical of Coady's approach. He had great enthusiasm and an entrepreneurial spirit which, combined with impatience, enabled him to get to the heart of problems, outline in broad detail what needed to be done, and then move on to fresh fields and new challenges. People like him are called social entrepreneurs today.

Leaving the convention, Coady returned to Antigonish to become the first director of St. F.X.'s Extension Department and to launch a social movement that would change the lives of thousands of people.

3

The Man and the Movement

We shall probably have to live dangerously, but that is one of
the great characteristics of leadership.

—Moses Coady

T he Halifax *Chronicle-Herald*, whose owner became a strong supporter of Coady's, welcomed the creation of St. F.X.'s Extension
Department and the priest's appointment to head it: "No better
man could be found for this important work," W.H. Dennis said. "He
is of the people and he has never lost the common touch with people,
their needs and ambitions." Canon Russell Elliott, an Anglican minister
who knew and was inspired by Coady, described him as "a man of the
community and the countryside [with] no place for social sophistication.
He had no polish and was not an academic." Coady did not force reality
into preconceived theories. He confronted the world as it was and strove
to change it through providing visions of a better life and supporting
and encouraging all who shared them. Alex Laidlaw, who worked with
him in the 1940s, identified one of Coady's main characteristics:

> He was a fervent democrat.... For him, the world had had
> enough of rule by a few strong men at the top. A new age
> would dawn, he believed, when the whole mass of humanity
> would lift itself to a new level of life, when democratic man
> would emerge.

His friend Mary MacNeil wrote of him:

Because he was so convinced that everyone he met was clever and well-intentioned, they did become so, to the limit of their capabilities. All those who knew him tried to be what he was so sure they were.

This big-hearted man realized that everyone had to see beyond the instruments of change – the co-ops, credit unions, buying clubs, lobster factories – reach into their own hearts and find there what they needed to change their lives and other people's. Laidlaw noted the "elements" in his friend: "Priest by vocation, philosopher by training, educator and teacher by profession, and social reformer by choice."

A lifelong Liberal in politics, he had the support of Angus L. Mac-Donald, Liberal premier of Nova Scotia from 1933 to 1940 and from 1945 to 1954. Conservative in theological matters, unlike Father Jimmy, Coady kept on the right side of the Catholic hierarchy. He sought nothing for himself, although he had an early penchant for fast cars and cigars. He lived in the campus room that he first occupied when he returned from Rome. He never lost the common touch, the ability to relate to others in ways and words they understood.

A Church in Turmoil

Coady never applied his co-operative principles to the Church. He was so deeply rooted in the Catholic tradition that the idea probably never came to him. The priest was for him the natural leader in the community who could help free people from the false imagination created by the dominant culture.

—Gregory Baum, *Catholics and Canadian Socialism: Political Thought in the Thirties and Forties*

In the late nineteenth century, the Vatican struggled to find a middle way between communism and capitalism as industrialization and urbanization accelerated in Europe. Marx and his followers promised heaven on earth through the dictatorship of the proletariat, while capitalists assured all that greater bliss would come in this life through increases in the production and consumption of material goods. In 1891, Pope Leo XIII issued the encyclical *On the Condition of the Working Classes* (*Rerum Novarum* – "Of New Things"), an attempt to point a way forward for the faithful. This document saw society in organic terms, as an inter-related whole, not a collection of individuals and groups. Liberal societies promoted individualism, while the pope emphasized interdependence among people. Increasingly, the powerful maintained their privileges while the "needy and powerless multitude" suffered. Employers used human beings as "instruments and treated labourers as things." Workers should be treated decently and paid a just wage so that they could support their families and live in dignity. While condemning communism, the pope defended the concept of private property, and claimed that the state should protect the rights of poor and helpless people. The encyclical endorsed the work of Social Catholics in forming "study conferences, mutual aid associations and labour organizations." It looked back to medieval times, when guilds and voluntary organizations brought people together and society operated as an organic entity.

Coady's vision of what he called "the good and abundant society" likewise saw the future in terms of the past, in the recreation of the kind of community in which he grew to manhood. Co-operation would replace conflict between classes.

In 1931, Pope Pius XI issued the encyclical *On Social Reconstruction* (*Quadragesimo Anno*) to mark the 40th anniversary of *Rerum Novarum*. It covered much of the same ground, affirming the dignity of all humans. Pius XI attacked capitalism and the greedy rich as well as communism, while continuing to support the concept of private property. He backed the work of Catholic social organizations and floated the idea of intermediary bodies that would bring people together for the common good and avoid the excesses of capitalism and state domination of the economy.

How much did these documents influence Coady's ideas and the work of the Antigonish Movement? Coady saw himself as a practical person, not an intellectual:

> The spiritual leaders – at least many of them – prefer to spend their time talking about abstract things like social justice, social charity, and democracy, that give them the feeling that they are doing something to justify their existence, when in reality they are cute apologists for the privileged status quo.

Coady practised what the Vatican preached, creating a network of intermediary bodies – co-operatives, credit unions and other ventures run by people at the community level. He believed that to change people's hearts, you had to create new economic institutions. Moral exhortations and official statements were no substitute for ventures that went beyond the concepts of charity and justice and helped marginalized people to be self-reliant and interdependent at the local level. Coady believed that the existing economic system was rotten, whether it was based on lais-sez-faire capitalism or communism. A new world, free of the ills of the old, would emerge when a new economic system, based on co-operation and consumer power, came into being.

Gregory Baum surveyed left-wing political thought in Canada between the two world wars. He concluded,

> The Antigonish movement was certainly the most original and daring response of Canadian Catholics to the social injustices during the Depression. It was based on an alternative vision of society, it was radical and went beyond the church teach-ings on several issues, advocated a religious materialism and introduced reforms in Canadian society that had explosive implications.... The movement also harboured paradoxes. Coady...was a radical and an activist deeply rooted in the Catholic tradition.

Some Catholic authorities were suspicious of anything that might be construed as radical thought. Father Harvey Steele, a Cape Bretoner inspired by Coady while studying at St. F.X. in the 1930s, recalled two such incidents.

At the Nova Scotia university, Steele had a small circle of friends and enjoyed the general camaraderie on campus. When he entered a seminary in Ontario in 1932, he became friendly with three other stu-dents and a young priest. The rector called him into his office and told him that particular friendships were strictly forbidden in the institution: "The principle was that it was extremely dangerous and inappropriate for anyone to form a strong and exclusive friendship with anyone else." *Quadrigesimo Anno*, with its plea that people be treated like human be-ings and that associations between them be encouraged, had not been interpreted by the rector as applying to his own men.

Another shock came when Steele spoke to a student about the conditions in the coal mines in Cape Breton. This man passed on what he had heard from Steele to other seminarians. The Cape Bretoner again found himself called on the carpet in the rector's office: "Is it true, Harvey, that you talked with a certain student and said that you were in favour of labour unions, credit unions and co-ops?" Steele readily admitted that he had. The rector bellowed at him that if he ever heard him "speak of things like that here, you will pack your bags and get out. There is no room in the priesthood for communists."

Coady, however, managed to keep what he was doing inside the Catholic tent, although it did push out some of the sides of it, and opened new entrances into it.

The Early Stages

Great events and great developments are sometimes caused by small things.

—Moses Coady

With A.B. MacDonald, Coady had seen what the leaders in adult education were doing in western Canada and the United States. A.B., born in Heatherton, Antigonish County, studied at the Ontario Agricultural College in Guelph and worked as an ag. rep. in Ontario and Nova Scotia. He was Inspector of Schools for Antigonish-Guysborough when Coady invited him to become assistant director of the new Extension Department.

A.B. agreed to take the job only if the leaders of the Catholic clergy in Cape Breton would support him. R.J. MacSween, also an ag. rep., took the train to Sydney and met with these "hard-headed Scotsmen." After convincing them that St. F.X. was committed to their cause, he returned on the late train. A.B. met him at the station. He still had his doubts about leaving the security of a government job for the untried field of adult education, but he said "yes" to Coady's offer.

His skills and abilities complemented Coady's. Tall, handsome, always beautifully dressed, A.B. also had the common touch and could be blunt and direct when the occasion demanded. Coady promoted the cause of adult education with his speeches at community meetings. A.B. followed up these presentations, helping interested listeners to organize co-ops and credit unions. He, too, was an impressive speaker.

As McSween put it, "What a team they were! Dr. Coady, learned, dynamic, impressive, yet humble, zealous and kind; A.B. charming, jovial and good natured, but at the same time ambitious, practical and with a rare genius for organization."

Early in 1929, Coady wrote to A.B., setting out "some high spots in my program.... I don't know if I can at the present moment outline to you a coherent programme of extension work. I have so many things on my mind that it is difficult to say which is the most practical to begin with." Impressed by what they had seen in western Canada, he stated, "First of all, we need organization by communities for educational purposes.

This would finally result in economic ventures.... Activities which lead to economic betterment will result in progress along cultural lines."

Coady's breadth of vision appears in his scheme for the new department: "We need broadcasting, circulating libraries, correspondence work, country-wide debates on vital topics, community scoring for efficiency purposes, etc., etc." Borrowing an idea from adult education work in the West, he proposed a scheme whereby "locals are formed and then federated for educational purposes. The central organization relays the proper knowledge to the people."

He threw in another idea, drawn from British experience, suggesting that a labour college would "create leaders for all groups of common men [and be] the culmination of the extension movement." At the University of Wisconsin, a leader in adult education with 40,000 students enrolled in various programs, faculty members took part in the work. Coady saw the need for "one or two good men to give their whole time to research in the economic and purely scientific fields.... Fact finding, or research...must parallel every movement for the betterment of the people."

Some of Coady's initial ideas did become realities, including a labour college. But the Extension Department never developed any capacity to do research. Faculty at St. F.X. gave popular lectures in the town; these met with little response and were discontinued.

In 1930, the director of St. F.X.'s Extension Department again put his methodical mind to work and came up with lists of proposed educational activities for it. He divided them into two categories: High School and College Credit Types, and Non-Credit Types.

Under the first category, Coady listed short courses, correspondence, study clubs, radio courses, the development of technical schools and folk schools and night schools. The second category included all of the above, plus general lectures, travelling libraries, home reading clubs, the provision of information through letters, circulars and pamphlets and the establishment of circulating libraries. Slides, art collections and films would be sent out to small communities, an idea Coady and A.B. picked up at the University of Alberta. The Department would publish a regular bulletin full of useful information to readers.

Coady drew up an extraordinary list of planned activities:

> Organizing (1) Country-wide debates on vital topics, essay and public speaking competitions. (2) Planning programs for Community Centres. (3) Rural community and town improve-

ment competitions. (4) Debating Clubs, Literary, Art and Dramatic Clubs, Recreational Clubs.

For a proponent of co-operation, there appears to be a heavy emphasis on competition. The statement continued: "Through some of these educational agencies young men and women of exceptional talent may be discovered, and assisted through scholarship." This had happened to Coady, and he wanted the same opportunities available to other bright young people.

There is no mention in the statement of how the Extension Department's work would relate to the ongoing efforts by the federal and provincial agencies already engaged in local economic development. Their fieldworkers supported Coady's efforts, but one story claims that officials sitting in government offices trembled when he entered them. The story is probably apocryphal for, above all, Coady was a kind man and no one had any reason to fear him.

The university allocated $10,535 to the Extension Department for its first year. Some of this money may have come from the Scottish Catholic Society; in later years, the department received grants from the Carnegie Corporation. But Coady was always short of funds. He took only $1,000 a year in salary from the first budget. A.B. received $4,000. "Periodicals, Open Shelf Library, Circulating Libraries and Visual Instruction" was allocated $1,575, and a quarter of the budget went for travelling expenses. Coady and A.B. knew that they would be on the road a great deal, and hired Kay Thompson as a "stenographer," for which she received $960 a year. Thompson, a local woman, had graduated from Mount St. Bernard, which was affiliated with St. F.X. (and on the same campus), and the Nova Scotia Teachers' College. She had moved to New York but was happy to come back and work for the Extension Department. In hiring her, Coady broke new ground. In the 1930s, women could be teachers, nurses or domestics, or work in offices in low-level positions.

Kay Thompson was the first of many women Coady hired and treated as equals. He gave them responsible positions and believed they could undertake any task. Thompson became more than a mere stenographer. She served as the department's anchor, bringing order into the chaos created by two enthusiastic men. In reality, Thompson was a pioneer adult educator.

Opening Guns

> There was a feeling of urgency, a spirit of aggressiveness, and
> a sense of great mission about it all.
>
> —Alex Laidlaw, *The Campus and the Community*

Coady and A.B. already had a network of contacts as they travelled around eastern Nova Scotia. When *Quadragesimo Anno* appeared in 1931, it stimulated lively debate in the Diocese of Antigonish. Whatever Coady and A.B. were doing, they seemed to be on the right track.

To be successful, a social movement has to have wide appeal. Its ideas must be accepted by gatekeepers in communities who see practical value in them. The two men from St. F.X. knew how to talk to these people and bring them onside. They also knew how to listen to those who told them about life at the local level, and about what was happening in communities that were being depleted by forces beyond their control. Not all priests welcomed Coady's arrival. In one community he was met by two residents who told him that the local priest had no interest in co-operation. But the movement began with a critical mass of dedicated disciples, including many priests in Acadian communities.

What became known as the "opening gun" of the Antigonish Movement, in Coady's words, was "fired" at a meeting in West Bay Road, Inverness County, on September 8, 1930. This event was carried out with the co-operation of field-workers from the provincial Department of Agriculture. Men like R.J. MacSween, J.C.F. MacDonnell and S.J. MacKinnon became unofficial members of the Antigonish Movement.

After this meeting, the idea of study clubs took hold. Coady did not have a staff who could go into communities to lead discussions and action, so he had to rely on native talent. Young men and women could develop their potential while they worked to enhance that of others. As a result of the Great Depression, which began in October 1929 with the Wall Street stock market crash, bright people no longer were migrating to the States in the same numbers; many of those who had done so lost their jobs and returned home. With few jobs available to them, they joined study clubs and started to work for their communities.

The Extension Department produced material for study clubs, issuing a mimeographed bulletin, *Some Fundamental Considerations.* People needed reliable information if they were to learn how to start and run new business ventures. From the beginning, the department focused on two themes – what it was trying to do and how people could solve their problems.

Coady's philosophy of education encouraged adults to find the information they needed to better their individual and collective lives. One of the first initiatives involved sending chapters of a textbook, *Making the Most of Agriculture,* to the leaders of study groups. It came with a letter:

> We shall branch out into more specialized studies in accordance with the wishes of our study groups. It should be borne in mind from the outset that our studies should all tend to the solution of the actual difficulties confronting us today.

Developing publications written in an accessible style for readers with limited literacy skills proved to be an ongoing challenge for the Antigonish Movement. Interested individuals and groups had access to a free circulating library in the Extension office, set up "to place at your disposal the very best literature on the subjects studied."

Coady wrote and spoke in dramatic terms; the leaders of the study groups were usually the most educated persons in the community and could communicate the information to their members. Thus the movement taught the teachers, who passed on what they learned to others. Today, this approach is known as "training the trainers." Coady and his colleagues stumbled upon ways of communicating information almost by accident. They did not have a corps of university specialists or trained adult educators standing by to assist. The women and men who received, read and disseminated the material from the Extension Department, managed to create, by trial and error, a critical mass of learners who discovered how to take knowledge to the people.

In time, the driving energy in the study clubs came from four simple prescriptions: "Listen! Study! Discuss! Act!" The Extension staff produced a series of pamphlets entitled *We Learn by Doing.* Coady wrote of these early days: "The idea of launching out into this movement was new and in those days revolutionary…. St. F.X. had little money…. A program such as was anticipated would naturally arouse opposition… It took courage to face the issue."

Coady had plenty of courage.

In the first hectic year of the movement, he addressed mass meetings, inspired his listeners, told them that their destiny was in their own hands, and encouraged them to form study groups and start learning how to tackle their problems with the available resources. He brought hope and optimism to a people mired in despair. He believed in the potential of ordinary people to change their world – and then the whole world. There was no need for pessimism! The highway to the good and abundant life was right in front of them. And the material for the study groups would provide signposts along the way.

Of course, the movement had to deal with skeptics and doubters because of its innovative approach to learning and its promise of changing the lives of poor, depressed and marginalized individuals and communities. But Coady had very few enemies. Nor did he encounter strong opposition, even from merchants. In part, this was due to the groundwork done by people like Father Jimmy, Little Doc MacPherson, and the ag. reps. and fisheries officers. But Coady's impressive physical presence, his credibility and formal qualifications, and his open-heartedness and generous spirit touched a wide range of people. This humble giant was driven by the need to help others, not by personal ambition. In the golden age of the movement, the slow-rising tide of prosperity generated by local effort lifted all boats – and the hearts and minds of all involved in this great endeavour.

The lack of capital for collective ventures at the local level began to concern Coady and his colleagues. Banks were not interested in lending money to poor people, and governments were strapped for cash and had little to offer self-help bodies. Father Jimmy had identified the need for a local system of pooling capital. At study group meetings, members collected nickels and dimes for local economic initiatives. But some sort of formal system was needed to accumulate capital from local sources on a regular basis and lend it out for collective business ventures.

The concept was not an unknown one. A chain of people's banks in Germany had helped the poor to better their lives. In 1900, Alphonse Desjardins had started the first caisse populaire in his home in Lévis, Quebec, aided by his wife, Dorimène. This initiative drew upon the experiences of the Farmers' Bank of Rustico, founded by Father Belcourt on Prince Edward Island in 1864 (it lost its charter in 1883). The caisse populaire movement, strongly supported by the local Catholic clergy, prospered, and in 1908 Desjardins went to Boston to advise Edward Filene, a philanthropist and department store owner, who was searching for ways to reduce the inequalities in American society. Filene also sought to combat usury to enable the poor to have more money for necessities. Filene had been impressed by the work of co-operative banks in India, and wanted Desjardins' advice on how to set up a similar scheme in the United States. After talking with the Canadian, Filene rejected terms like "people's banks" and "co-operative banks" to describe local savings and loans ventures. He preferred "credit union," and saw these bodies as a way of enabling the poor to save money rather than simply offering them credit to make prudent purchases to improve their standard of living and share in the rising prosperity of America. Filene's ideas, unlike those of Father Jimmy on economic democracy and local self-reliance, were implemented in private companies, where enlightened employers offered them to their workers as a fringe benefit. These ventures proved successful, and by 1920, four states had 190 credit unions. Then Roy Bergengren became involved in the movement and served as its prime mover. A lawyer who had served as an officer in the American army during the First World War, he had failed in the candy business. At one time he had done work for Filene, and sought him out for advice on his future. The merchant offered him the job of managing the Massachusetts credit union movement from an office in Boston.

Efforts had been made by A.B. MacDonald and others in 1925 to introduce credit unions in Nova Scotia. At a farmers' meeting in Bridgewater in that year, MacDonald, seconded by H.H. Cutton, secured passage of a motion urging the passing of a credit union act as the first step in the process. Bergengren's advice to those interested in starting credit unions was always "Get the act."

A.B. had the right idea, but the wrong timing. A bill was drafted for Nova Scotia, and the legislature's agricultural committee reported favourably on it. But it failed to gain approval and died on the order paper.

In 1931, as Bergengren prepared to leave on vacation, "a little priest came bustling into the office." Father Jimmy wanted the American's help in starting credit unions in Nova Scotia. Bergengren talked over the request with Filene, "who pointed out that we had more than we could handle in the United States." Father Jimmy must have been very persuasive, though, because Bergengren decided to give up most of his vacation to visit Nova Scotia, "which was to become a second home in my affections."

On September 1, 1931, he spoke at an evening session of the Diocesan Rural Conference, impressing everyone with his knowledge, sincerity and dedication to the credit union movement. The next day, Coady drove the visitor to Canso, "where we had a fine meeting in a motion-picture theatre."

Then Father Jimmy took Bergengren to Little Dover. Climbing on the stern of a beached boat, the priest began "to wave his arms like a miniature windmill." Fishermen assembled "and we had a rally, the first time to my knowledge that the credit union was ever discussed in Nova Scotia at a meeting of the people." These encounters showed the difference between Coady's structured approach to learning, and that of his cousin, who relied on spontaneity and took every opportunity to generate interest in new ideas.

Coady inspired Bergengren to write his book, *Crusade: The Fight for Economic Democracy in North America: 1921–1945*. He quotes a favourite maxim of Coady's several times in the work: "For the people can do ten times what they think they can do." Bergengren adds, "When Father Coady discovered how much more we can do than we think we can do to hasten the final object of the Crusade, he reached for us one of the great permanent milestones along the way which chart human progress."

Coady told the American of his vision of the good life. Leaders went beyond setting up savings-and-loans ventures. With A.B., he taught Bergengren that "co-operative credit is but part of the co-operative whole." Bergengren also noted the division of labour in the leadership of the Extension Department. Coady was "the born leader and militant modern prophet," while A.B. "goes into the highways and byways to make practical preachments of co-operation by effective organization."

In May 1932, the Nova Scotia government passed legislation for the establishment of credit unions.

That winter, Bergengren came to Antigonish to help in the creation of the province's first credit union. As he prepared to leave, Coady gave him a big coonskin coat and insisted that the American try it on. "I was lost in it. I tried to convince him that I didn't want it." Coady's response was blunt: "Take it. Where you are going you will need it." Driving through a rising storm, the three men headed for Little Dover. The weather worsened as they pressed on to Inverness, on the west coast of Cape Breton Island, where Bergengren tried to sleep in an unheated bedroom: "I hadn't been in bed long before my teeth began to chatter." Then he noticed Coady's coat, put it on, and "slept warm and comfortable." Coady, meanwhile, travelled on to Reserve Mines. Bergengren accompanied A.B. to the schoolhouse in Broad Cove in a car that had lost its windows. He saw people struggling through snowdrifts in the same direction as the car was heading. Where were they going on such a vile day? he asked A.B. "That's our audience!" came the reply. Bergengren recalled:

The organization of the first credit union in Nova Scotia, in the little schoolhouse in Broad Cove, where we huddled about that roaring fire in the old stove while the storm howled outside and tried to get in, was probably the high spot of the credit union movement in North America in 1932.

These pioneers named their new venture after Edward Filene. The two men went back to Inverness that evening for another meeting, and then drove to Reserve Mines. Here, Coady had prepared the way, and 36 people signed up for the credit union: "Everyone there would have signed, but the white space at the bottom of the blank gave out." Then A.B. and Bergengren organized a "typical industrial credit union" for the employees of Eastern Light and Power in Sydney. Bergengren returned to Nova Scotia nine more times to advise on the credit union movement: the one in Antigonish is named after him. He always remembered the kindness of Coady: "It was typical [of him] to give me his coat."

With the establishment of the first credit union, and the indigenous tradition of co-ops, Coady and the movement had two instruments for mobilizing people, pooling their savings and turning them into participants in their own economic and social development.

In 1933, Coady had a clear idea of the way ahead. In the first issue of *The Extension Bulletin*, dated November 7, 1933, he laid out "the balanced plan of self-help," as the movement he led entered a new phase. In 1932, 179 study clubs had 1,500 members, and eight credit unions and two co-op stores had been founded. In the following year, the number of study clubs had almost doubled, to 350, and membership in them nearly tripled, to 5,250. Nineteen credit unions had been formed, four co-op stores started, and eleven co-op fish and lobster plants created.

Coady's article in the *Bulletin* started by defending the movement:

> There are those in nearly every section who will slander group study and group action applied to solving the pressing economic problems of the people. One of the most ill-born slanders seeks to identify economic co-operation with communism or revolutionary socialism. This error is promoted by persons with selfish motives.

The priest reached back into his past in the Margaree for an image to convey his message. The slanderers were clinging to the rooftops, "idly unaware that such a large segment of humanity is going down with the torrent."

Then he asked:

What is Co-operation? It is a plan by which the people learn
to produce the goods which their locality permits through
group effort; it embraces group buying, group selling, group
financing, and so on for all the social services which shield
the welfare of men. It opposes the system of man set against
man in competitive fury for livelihood.

Quadragesimo Anno had condemned both capitalism and communism and sought an unspecified middle path. Coady pointed out that
he was following this route. A co-operative lobster factory in Dover
that had divided $1,000 among its members "is not a centre of com-
munism." He stressed, "Self-help by the people isn't communism, nor
is it unrestricted capitalism. Instead it is the sane middle way, utilizing
the best of these."

Coady highlighted themes that would be reiterated in all his
speeches and writings: "Nothing was ever built yet on theory alone."
He discussed consumer power, a topic that would obsess him because
he saw there a way for everyone and anyone to influence how the economic system worked.

A first requisite...in a just economic order, is a just form of
the distribution of goods. We are all consumers. Every man,
woman and child is a consumer. It has been customary to allow
our consumer needs to be served by individuals for profit ...
tending drastically, of late years to chain store dictation and
monopoly control of prices.

This system of control could be broken by consumers managing
the buying and distribution of the goods they use: "They should operate their own stores." From this premise, Coady built up a picture of
a consumer-run co-operative society. Through group ownership and
operation of industry, people would run industries to supply their own
needs and sell the surplus: "Local industries, proper to the community,
operated by the people, allowing the profits to remain at home, is the
second great step in a workable economy."

The third factor required for economic generation "is a system of
credit for the people." Credit unions would encourage thrift and help
people to learn how to handle financial matters while making credit
available for local needs. The fourth step in a balanced plan of self-help
was group marketing.

In time, farmers could capture Nova Scotia's urban markets "which they have lost by dependence on brokers and by the decay that follows on blind competitive selling." Farmers were encouraged to co-operate to secure better prices for their products.

Coady assured his readers:

> The people inspired to work out their own vital problems through these four co-operative avenues pursued simultaneously, will lift themselves out of the abject dependence to which the competitive system has reduced them. They will thus become self-supporting, freed from the bondage of political patronage, and from dole-slavery to the state. They will, in fact, be the making of the state.

He had an astonishing vision of the new world that would come into being if everyone followed his four-fold path: Listen. Study. Discuss. Act. "For it is by self-help associations that this country can escape the mongrel form of socialism into which it is rapidly descending, because of the scandalous default of private business in supplying livelihoods."

With their livelihoods assured, "people come automatically to the point where they may deal with the fifth realm, [that of] of social welfare ... what forms of property should be reserved to the state, old age pensions, social insurance, and related forms of economic discipline which shield the common welfare."

In the years to come, Coady would see a great flowering of co-ops, credit unions and collective ventures. He would continue to propound his vision of the good and abundant society based on the four principles he outlined in 1933. And he would become increasingly testy as people fell short of his expectations and failed to create the bright new world he had envisaged.

4

The Barnstorming Years

There is a tide in the affairs of men
Which, taken at the flood, leads on to fortune;
Omitted, all the voyage of their life
Is bound in shallows and in miseries.
—William Shakespeare, *Julius Caesar*, Act V, Scene III

A s the tide of the Great Depression swept more and more people into a bottomless abyss of fear, hopelessness and despair, the Antigonish Movement offered them a way of gaining some control over their lives. Competitive individualism offered no solutions to the increasing economic chaos and disorder. Only through collective action could people save themselves and their communities.

Coady's message of a new world created through self-help fell on receptive ears. By 1938, 1,110 study groups involved 10,000 members in discussions about the future of their communities. Credit unions numbered 142, and 78 other co-operative ventures had been formed. In 1932, the movement entered the strife-torn industrial scene in Cape Breton by opening an office in Glace Bay, and another in Sydney in the following year.

These numbers and the activities of Coady and his colleagues are impressive. But they are small in scale compared to the mainstream business sector. Something else emerged from the study clubs and co-operatives, a feature of social movements much harder to measure than the number of their enterprises. When you talk with the men and women who participated in the Antigonish Movement, their voices soften and their eyes light up.

They look back at their time with Coady and his people as great years in their lives. They were not doing good works among the poor or struggling to define community development. They had their feet on the ground and their heads in the air, inspired by a remarkable group of men and women leaders who showed them how to blend personal development with the advancement of the collective good.

Coady's Way

> We are still bubbling over with enthusiasm, although we have lots of problems, but the general situation is very promising.
>
> —Moses Coady

The word "enthusiasm" derives from the Greek meaning "the God inside." This was the key to Coady's style of speaking and acting as he set out to break the culture of silence and to change the mindsets of his listeners. The Antigonish Movement developed a specific way of organizing people for action. When Coady addressed a public meeting, as one listener put it, "Once you heard him, you could never be the same." He sent his audiences home "to think for weeks about the things he said."

At first, the people who came to the meetings had difficulties with his style of address. As Coady recalled, "The people were, in the beginning, incredulous. It was like talking to a mountain where one heard nothing but the echo of his voice." But the seeds of co-operation had already been sown in some communities by dedicated priests, and Coady could inspire people to act. In Grand Etang, Father Joseph DeCoste, "an old College mate of mine, a brilliant and good man" put up his insurance policy to buy a lobster factory for the local fishermen.

Coady developed an interesting way of addressing audiences. He began hesitantly, as if unsure of what he was about to say. The audience became restless, wondering why they had come to hear this inarticulate individual. Coady sometimes created resentment at meetings by his blunt way of talking about the evils of society and accusing his listeners of being responsible for their own plight. Slowly, he summoned up his oratorical powers and began to focus on a topic he knew to be of local interest. Why were things as they were? he asked. And if something was damaging the community, why was this so – and why was it permitted to persist? What could be done to change things, to give people more control over their individual and collective lives? Soon the audience became entranced, spellbound, excited about what he had to say.

Coady had the knack of turning abstract concepts into simple, easily understood, concrete examples of what was wrong with the world and what could be done about it. He spoke in parables, in crystal clear language. In his youth, he told his listeners, he had seen the Margaree River in flood, driving the muskrats from their riverbank burrows, drowning many of them. In the same way, the economic crash of 1929 had swept over the land, drowning people and their communities. The "orthodox economists and financiers" had no idea how to cope with these disasters. Coady told his audiences that credit unions and co-ops offered them a way to stem the flood and begin to change their lives through their own efforts.

Local ventures had to be efficiently run. Coady compared faltering co-ops to sick lambs. Like them, they should be nursed back to health by the community.

Thus began what Coady called his "double-barrelled" approach to change, blending adult education and co-operation. He described his techniques as follows:

> It was a good thing that we were poor. We found a better technique by facing the actual situation and planning a way by which people could be mobilized to think, to study and get enlightenment.... The discussion circle...did not involve teachers; it was in line with our whole co-operative idea; we would make education part of the self-help movement; the people would come together by themselves and discuss their problems.

This process would be known today as consciousness-raising or creating awareness. Coady wanted the talk at the community level to result in action – not more talk. The first logical step in the adult education process was "to round up the people, so to speak." Through the press and the pulpit people came together: "At the first meetings fundamental, homely philosophies were placed before the people." They were told that progress came through the operation of the mind "and that mind counted much more than muscle." Then people were told of "the great possibilities for life around them everywhere, if they would only condition themselves to the point where they could realize them." Examples of self-help ventures by others were described.

Coady admitted that people "can be educated by books and the information they themselves gather, but philosophy and ideas come and go by human beings." After the mass meetings, study clubs were formed. A leader was selected by the group to serve as secretary, round up people, and ensure that they received the Extension Department's literature and attended meetings.

The small study clubs met once a month in a larger group, an associated or federated study club that served as a common meeting ground where people could talk about their difficulties and problems. Recreational and cultural activities took place at these meetings, and inspirational speakers addressed participants. "This direct and purposeful organization of the people is a short-cut to results," wrote Coady.

In the 1920s and 1930s, extension courses at universities were formal, stodgy and bureaucratic. Coady realized that adult education could be fun and did all he could to ensure that morale remained high while people worked out the solutions to their own problems. As he wrote, "If we had had money behind us we'd have taken the old way of doing it, which would be correspondence, and sending out lecturers to lecture on travels to Europe or something like that – some high-faluting stuff."

Study group members could also attend conferences of two kinds, vocational and general, to learn about what others were doing. As Coady put it, "The vocational conferences were meetings of representatives of all groups engaged in a given profession." Fishermen, farmers and industrial workers came together to discuss common concerns. Each year a general conference was held to air shared educational, social and economic problems. This process "finally culminated in a great institution, the Rural and Industrial Conference, which met annually in Antigonish" until war broke out in 1939. People came from all across Canada, the United States and other countries to these conferences, which attracted 1,200 participants in one year. *The New York Times* and the *Times of London* covered these meetings. On August 1, 1936, the latter asked: "How many of the educated and intelligent people who read this Supplement have ever heard of Antigonish?... Yet, amid the multitude of crowded experience, nothing moved me so much as the extramural work of the University of St. Francis Xavier, Antigonish!"

Alex Laidlaw describes Coady as the "chief guide and mentor of the work for over thirty years ... the integrator of the various inputs and resources ... its ablest interpreter." The Antigonish Movement could easily have been "a milk-and-water affair, with nothing to stir men's hearts and imagination" without Coady's spirit and courage. He became a father figure who "took considerable pride in his guerilla role in a war for social and economic change."

Coady did not hesitate to intervene at the local level if things did not go the way he wanted. Study groups, which usually had six to twelve members, had to act. One study group had been meeting all winter. Spring was coming when Coady dropped in for a visit. Everyone agreed "we have to decide to take some actions." Coady leapt up. "Lock the door!" he cried. "No one leaves until we decide to do something." A decision was reached, and "People threw their hats in the air and went home to tell their wives."

Nurturing New Leaders

> It is discouraging to find that great sectors of the common people themselves and some of their leaders are so unmindful of the spirit of our democratic ancestors that they will give in without any fight to the propaganda against programs that would mean a new life for them.
>
> —Moses Coady

It was several years before Coady acquired funds to hire more staff at the Extension Division. In following what he called "the pauper's way" of adult education, he had to find talent at the local level wherever he could. In the study groups, held in kitchens, church halls, rectories and other places, new leaders emerged. Coady advised his listeners to "do the evident, feasible things first. Begin where you are." The study group leaders were those who could grasp his vision of a new society and motivate people to act on immediate problems. Credit unions, which A.B. MacDonald described as being "as handy as a pocket in a shirt," provided a practical starting point for pooling spare cash in communities. Co-op ventures were more difficult to organize. Some communities moved into action fairly quickly after study groups identified viable business opportunities. Others held discussions for up to two years before creating a collective venture.

The Extension Department published *Credit Unions*, a pamphlet by Joseph MacIsaac, which contained questions and answers on these ventures. Study group leaders used it to work through the processes required to bring credit unions into being and to run them efficiently. Fieldworkers from the Extension Department addressed concerns not covered in the pamphlet. A.B. travelled to every community where meetings were

A family portrait, c. 1910. Front row, centre and right: Moses Coady's parents. Coady is in the back row; the other two women in the photograph are his cousins.

Moses Coady as a seminarian in Rome, c. 1905–1910

Moses Coady's home in the Margaree, c. 1950s

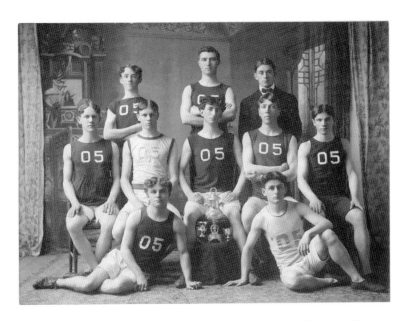

Moses Coady (centre, back row) and the St. Francis Xavier
University basketball team, c. 1904

Coady's cousin Fr. Jimmy Tompkins, c. 1930s

Dr. Coady with United Maritime Fishermen (UMF) representatives in Gander, Newfoundland, c. 1940s

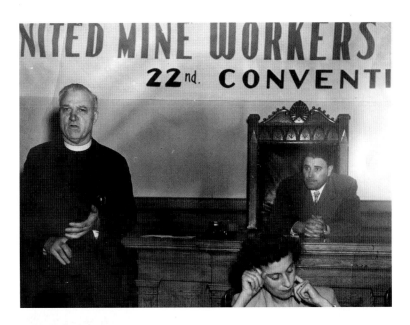

Dr. Coady speaking at a United Mine Workers convention c. 1947

Dr. Coady attending a Nova Scotia Credit Union Congress at St. F.X., 1951. From left: R.J. MacSween, A.B. MacDonald, Coady, and Ed O'Meara.

Panel of Antigonish Movement display, created by Sister Irene Doyle, CSM (Sr. Mary Anselm), to be presented to the pope for the Marian year 1950.

Coady Credit Union, New Aberdeen, Cape Breton, early 1950s

Dr. Coady with foreign students in the old Extension Department library at St. F.X., c. 1949–1950

Dr. Coady with Extension Department staff and visitor at Margaree Harbour, Cape Breton. From left: Ellen Arsenault, Dr. Coady, Sally Fraser, and an unknown visitor.

Dr. Coady gets ready for 1954 Convocation at St. F.X.

Sydney and St. F.X. Extension Department Staff, 1956. Front row, from left: Ellen Arsenault, Sally Fraser, Sr. Marie Michael MacKinnon, Dr. Coady, Alex Laidlaw, unidentified woman, Theresa MacKinnon, Ellen Pugh. Back row from left: Fr. Andy Hogan, Joe Laben, Monsignor Michael MacKinnon, Fr. George Topshee, John Chisholm, Rev. Dr. Dan MacCormick.

held to ensure that everything was in place for founding a credit union. The emerging leaders in the co-op and credit union movement thus had excellent support as they worked through the details of setting up new community organizations.

Coady recognized that the key to economic and social change lay in restructuring relationships between individuals. This process could not be conjured out of the air. It had to be nurtured by men and women who had the respect of community residents and the skills needed to serve the collective good, rather than their own personal interests. Such people formed part of what is today called the social capital of communities. Coady noted,

> The St.Francis Xavier Extension Department was fortunate that it found many ready-made leaders all over the country. The work was not going very long, however, when it became evident that something would have to be done to create a greater number of leaders.

As with other aspects of the work of the movement, leadership training was not something that Coady initially planned. In nurturing new leaders, however, he was replicating his own experiences. He was a bright young man from a rural area who had been given access to the best minds of his generation. What had worked for him and enabled him to serve his people more effectively would surely work for others.

In 1933, the Extension Department started courses for leaders on the St. F.X. campus:

> Men and women came in from all over the country for four weeks each year. In these courses the whole philosophy of co-operation and adult education was presented. The school was turned into a miniature society and all discussion techniques were tried out. The little discussion circle, or study club, was tried. Forum and panel discussions were added. The conference technique was featured. These men and women went back to their respective communities with a new enthusiasm for the work.

Between 1933 and 1939, 735 men and women took part in these leadership training sessions. As Coady put it,

> It is safe to say that no phase of the adult education work carried on by the Extension Department produced greater results. Scores of men and women who have since figured

prominently in the movement got their start and inspiration in these courses.

Coady had the knack of spotting indigenous talent, and great respect for ordinary people and what they knew. A staff member recalled a farmer, a man with very little formal education, leaving Coady's office. Coady remarked, "That's one of the wisest men I ever met." Again and again he told his listeners, "You can get the good life. You're poor enough to want it and smart enough to get it."

During the war, the Extension Department offered four-day "short courses" in communities in the Maritimes because people could not leave their homes to come to St. F.X. These proved effective in nurturing new leaders. Coady noted, "One of the great revelations of this short course was the finding of men and women who had only ordinary education, yet on account of their native ability and zeal they have gone on and educated themselves."

The Extension Department fed the new leaders a steady stream of informative pamphlets, brochures and short study guides. Some of the first mimeographed materials on buying clubs, marketing pools, credit, the history of co-operation and other topics were derived from periodicals and textbooks, but over time, the staff began to create their own publications. *The Extension Bulletin* was "published in the interests of adult education," according to its masthead. The first issue carried Coady's piece on balanced self-help and outlined its goal in starting "a new departure in our method of carrying education direct to the people." The *Bulletin* would offer "a more coherent and sustained course of studies.... Its function is going to be largely suggestive and stimulating." Extension students should do "considerable subsidiary reading.... Articles should be studied in private and discussed at study club meetings."

Coady appointed George Boyle, a professional writer, to edit *The Extension Bulletin* in 1936, and claimed that the publication was "going to become so dazzling that you will have to put on smoked glasses to read it." Sections of the paper included Education, Economic Studies, Credit Studies, Fishermen's Affairs, and The Woman's Page. In subsequent years, a Labour Forum and The Farm Study Club were added. Ten thousand copies of the bulletin were printed, and in May 1939, it was renamed *The Maritime Co-operator* as the movement spread across the region.

The Extension Department also produced pamphlets. Many were reprints of speeches given by Coady and others at conferences. Other pamphlets covered study clubs, the worker as consumer, credit unions, "Be

Your Own Banker," "Shopping Basket Economics," "The Middle Way," and economic democracy and co-operativism in Sweden and Denmark.

In his first circular to study clubs in 1930, Coady stated:

> It should be borne in mind from the very outset that our studies should all tend to the solution of the actual difficulties confronting us today. When we master the fundamental business principles and discover our economic possibilities, then the actual work of undertaking business ventures in line with our certain conclusions will soon be in order.

His vision of a new order of society did not prevent him from taking a hard-nosed approach to the creation of the new business ventures that would underpin it. He had seen co-operatives in Nova Scotia fail because not enough preparation had been done before setting them up, and ongoing education had been neglected. His way was different. Careful thought and discussion had to go into planning co-operative ventures. And the new leaders who emerged from the study groups had to be kept informed. Laidlaw summed up the role of the Extension Department in the 1930s:

1) It supplied the educational basis that was to a great extent lacking up to that time.

2) It greatly speeded up the organization of new societies.

3) It introduced new types of organizations that were not in existence before.

4) It united all kinds of organizations in a people's movement and gave them a sense of social purpose.

The Women of the Antigonish Movement

> It was a wonderful experience. We knew we were involved in something greater than ourselves and that was a source of great satisfaction. We would not have missed it for anything.
>
> —Sister Irene Doyle

In quoting her colleague Ida Delaney, another member of Coady's staff said that "she spoke for all of us." Coady believed in the potential of women, and particularly encouraged them to play leadership roles in his movement. He helped the Sisters of Saint Martha to secure more autonomy from St. F.X., and involved them in his school in the Margaree.

In 1932, Father Jimmy had coaxed the sisters into a new role by involving them in community social work in Canso. Coady claimed that if he had 50 Marthas, he could change the world. In February 1930, after his fact-finding tour of adult education programs, Coady visited the nuns' residence at Bethany. He was "chock full of progressive ideas" and gave "a wonderful lecture on co-operation." The sisters "found it hard to go through [the] ordinary routine of going to bed after the lecture was over." Addressing novices on another occasion, Coady told them, "You have to be blow torches and set fires." At the rural conference at St. F.X. in 1931, the idea of forming women's study clubs and co-operating with bodies such as the Women's Institute arose. In the following year, Coady asked Mother Ignatius, the superior of the Marthas, for her advice on the best way of starting women's discussion circles and the kinds of books the members would need. In 1932, Coady received $35,000 from the Carnegie Corporation. He could now hire more staff. In August 1933, Mother Ignatius appointed Sister Marie Michael MacKinnon to Extension. She came from Father Michael Gillis's parish in Boisdale, Cape Breton, and had studied home economics in Quebec before entering the congregation. This highly intelligent young woman had just graduated from St. F.X. that year, receiving the Governor General's medal for the highest aggregate in her class. Coady, A.B. and Kay Thompson went to Bethany to invite her to form women's study clubs. A record of the meeting noted, "A program was outlined." When Sister Marie Michael joined the Extension Department at a salary of $1,000 a year, neither Coady nor A.B. gave her a detailed blueprint for her new job. She later recalled that Coady created an "environment of freedom and trust, and of support...which gave us a confidence we should never otherwise have had." The nun flourished in this atmosphere. Within a year, she had set up 300 women's study clubs to discuss homemaking, rural recreation, handicrafts and co-op organization.

The clubs proved popular. In one community, a local leader pushed her father's car out of the garage and the members created a place of their own. Credit unions found ready acceptance among rural women. Many handled the money in their families and knew the perils of weak husbands who spent their wages on drink and gambling. The women also knew all about debt; some had to be "carried" by local merchants when they did not have the cash to pay the grocery and other bills. Interest soon began to mount and indebtedness increased. The Extension Department had a slogan: "We don't buy goods at the credit union and you should not buy credit at the [co-op] store."

Sister Marie Michael edited the women's page in *The Extension Bulletin*, wrote articles for it, attended conferences, and became an articulate spokeswoman for the work of Extension. She later earned a library degree and turned the Extension Department's library into a "joyous place." She carried Coady's message to a wide range of audiences. At the 1938 Rural and Industrial Conference, she stated, "Women must be thoroughly imbued with vision of a better world and the means to obtain it."

Coady first met Sister Anselm (Irene) Doyle, who came from Melford in Inverness County, in 1930. He drove her to Bethany. Had she ever been in a car like this before? he asked her. When she said she had not, he asked her if she'd like to see the Buick travel really fast and then proceeded to go 60 miles an hour over the rough road to Antigonish. The novice completed a Bachelor of Science in Home Economics at St. F.X. in 1935, and was seconded to the Extension Department. She plunged into the work there, doing secretarial tasks, travelling to women's study clubs, and turning her hand to any and every task needed to keep the department's office running efficiently. She had an astute assessment of Coady: "He was a little boy in one way. He always had his shoes polished and his hat brushed to perfection. Sometimes he'd say, 'See my new shoes' or call attention to a new suit." Sister Marie Michael said of her colleague that she "could more than hold her own in any skirmish that might occur."

Coady created a family atmosphere in the Extension office and the women on his staff flourished. He continually sought ideas and input from his staff. He would refer to himself as "Little Mosie from Margaree" and was delighted when Sister Irene Doyle spoke about him in that way. The women humanized their charismatic leader, who delegated authority to them and let them get on with their jobs.

Sister Marie Michael encountered a situation that throws a great deal of light on how the other members of her congregation saw the movement. Knowing that Coady was often accused of radicalism, the novices staged a mock trial of Sister Marie. She was accused of "spreading seeds of communism throughout the country and trying to form a Soviet Government." After being found guilty, Sister Marie was sentenced to judge a subsequent debate.

The history of the order says this of the two sisters:

> They found the extension office a stimulating and exciting place to work. The office staff developed a strong spirit of family and co-operation. And Coady, who valued the opinions of all, male and female, regularly appeared in a state

of excitement and exhilaration over promising new ideas
and developments. His enthusiasm was infectious. All these
connections, both formal and informal, between the St. F.X.
extension office and the congregation affected the sisters. No
doubt it developed among them broad social concerns, new
types of skills, and intimacy with Maritime people and their
economic and social problems.

In 1936, Ida Gallant, a teacher, joined the Extension Department.
Coady sent her to the Glace Bay office to work with Alex MacIntyre,
the tough ex-miner who ran it. Gallant, the only female staff member
to write her story of the movement, eventually married John Delaney,
the international board member for District 26 of the United Mine
Workers of America. Gallant travelled around the region to meet with
co-operators as well as running Extension's Glace Bay office. In 1937,
another woman joined Coady's staff. Zita O'Hearn had just received her
master's degree in English from St. F.X. Coady met her on the street
and hired her. Sister Irene Doyle described O'Hearn as having "a sharp
analytical wit. [She] likes to take apart what she sees as distortions of
the truth." The newcomer became editor of *The Maritime Co-operator* and
also freelanced for other publications, helping to spread the word about
the movement.

Coady's knack for finding talent proved particularly useful when
the miners in Reserve Mines asked how to start and run a housing co-
operative, something about which he knew nothing. Two American
women experienced in this field came to Antigonish in 1937 with an
American Co-operative League study tour. Mary Elliott Arnold and Ma-
bel Reed had helped to found Consumer Co-operative Services in New
York. Political squabbles in the organization had eroded their faith in
the co-op movement and they came to Nova Scotia to have it renewed.
Coady's enthusiasm touched the two visitors, and they agreed to go to
Reserve Mines and work with Father Jimmy, who was the parish priest
there, and eleven miners and their wives to build co-operative housing.
This project became known as Tompkinsville. Arnold developed a great
affection for Coady. In 1939 she wrote to him, "The road to the stars
always seems smoother after I have talked with you." Ten years later when
his health had deteriorated, she wrote, "Above everything else, take care
of yourself. This is a pretty troublesome world and we have only one Dr.
Coady." Both Tompkins and Coady admired strong-minded women like
Arnold. She involved the wives of the miners in planning and building

the housing co-operative, although the deeds for the homes were all in the names of the men.

Although Arnold got along fine with Coady, Tompkins and the miners and their wives, she had difficulties with A.B., who she felt was not supportive of her efforts in organizing co-operative housing. He later eliminated it from the Extension program.

The two women left Nova Scotia in 1939. Arnold became chair of the Committee on Industrial Housing in the Co-operative Union.

The Movement at Its Peak

> A new Moses ... modest, mild-mannered and inspiring, greatest
> and most practical speaker I ever heard
>
> —A report on Coady's address to the
> American Country Conference, November, 1932

The writer of this report went on to claim that Coady had "the most profound but workable philosophy of life and therefore the most far-reaching message that I ever heard on any like occasion." Coady held "the hope of social justice before the eyes of the Conference."

The mention of social justice touches a responsive chord in our time, when the Catholic Church and numerous secular agencies claim to be working on its behalf. However, Coady never used what he saw as vague, abstract, feel-good terms like "social justice." Father Harvey Steele, ordained in 1936, noted in his autobiography, *Dear Old Rebel*,

> It is strange how some people, and not others, are grabbed
> by this virtue, justice. Always at the bottom of the Catholic
> virtues, it was never mentioned in the seminary training of my
> time. Pope Leo XIII...was the first pope to mention it. Ever
> since, popes have been mentioning it, but such pronounce-
> ments have been taken seriously by few bishops and priests.
> How could they understand? They lead affluent lives and were
> never told in their seminary days that justice is important.

Coady realized that there was little use talking in abstract terms if people had no control over their own lives. Economic development based on creating a greater degree of self-reliance in communities had to come first. Once people had a comfortable level of life, then discussions could focus on other topics. Meanwhile, Coady carried his vision, message and practical ideas to a wide range of audiences. One of his listeners spoke of the air having "a messianic effect."

His enthusiasm sustained his colleagues and impressed everyone. An address to the Rotary Club of New Glasgow was described in *The Eastern Chronicle* as "the most practical, the most useful and the best that the writer has listened to in these trying times. It should be repeated from every housetop." Coady drove himself hard in the early days of the movement. Between October 1 and 12, 1933, he spoke in sixteen communities in Cape Breton and in seven in mainland Nova Scotia. In the same month, he also gave speeches in Montreal, Ottawa, Kingston, Toronto, Calgary, St. Paul and Chicago. His physical stamina stood him in good stead on these exhausting trips over rough country road and in cramped airplanes.

While Coady and A.B. travelled, talked, inspired and organized, the women at the Extension office worked hard to support them and to service the growing number of study clubs and self-help ventures. Sisters Marie Michael and Irene Doyle gathered from anywhere and everywhere pamphlets, clippings, books and information that they thought would be useful to readers. Kay Thompson sorted through the mass of material and mimeographed excerpts for study clubs and courses. She attached a note to one box of publications: "I had to come up for air a few times while I was buried in this mountain of paper."

Coady recognized the value of their work and the fact that they were overburdened. From time to time, he would pile his staff into his big Buick and take them to the Margaree for some rest and relaxation. They picked strawberries and ate good country food. Coady could be thoughtless when he visited relatives, however. He relished the roast lamb dinners prepared by Katie, wife of his brother Joe. Before arriving at their home, he would write, "Dear Katie, I'm going home Sunday and will be there for dinner. I'll have four friends with me. Please have fresh lamb with all the trimmings." He asked for meals with maragans (a dish resembling haggis) and isbeans (a type of sausage) and other homemade foods. A friend noted, "He seemed to have little awareness of the problem that preparing a gourmet meal on...short notice could pose for...the wife of a farmer."

As the movement flourished, optimism rose in the region. In February 1935, *The Casket* reported: "We are all beginning to feel that our problems are not insurmountable at all." Roy Bergengren saw the study clubs as the key to the success of the movement:

> The very fact that such meetings can be held on this continent proves the priceless gift of freedom. In too many countries, if such meetings were held, the secret police would be knocking

at the door and arresting members of the group for harbour-
ing and discussing thoughts which might be dangerous to the
totalitarian state.

Through discussion and collective action, old tensions began to
dissolve and new partnerships formed.

Billy Tom Feltmate of Whitehead organized a fishermen's co-op.
Within three months "we brought the price of twine down from 70
cents to 27 cents; laths from $7.50 to $3.50 a thousand; gasoline from
40 cents to 26 1/2 cents." Relationships with neighbouring communities
also changed radically:

> Over in Port Felix, and previous to our organization there was
> a fence line, so to speak, between us, and each fellow kept
> to his own side of it. Protestant one side, and Catholic the
> other. We had no business transactions in any way. Since we
> fishermen began to organize and co-operate, we have become
> fast friends.

Coady's head and heart had created a social movement through
which people saw themselves in a different light: not as poor, oppressed
fishermen but as full human beings capable of organizing their own
affairs and working with anyone committed to the common cause. As
Billy Tom put it, "The story of how I fought through the Depression is
not my story alone. It is the story of hundreds of fishermen who fought
through with me."

In 1932, the people of Judique formed twelve study clubs. Two
years later they built a lobster factory. Canned lobsters brought better
returns than fresh groundfish that had to be sold to buyers on the wharf
for any price they cared to offer. The 30 members of the Judique lobster
co-op paid off the cost of their factory in two years. They built another
one, then opened a credit union and a co-op shop. The residents of
the community told Coady's staff that they were "much richer than we
were a decade ago, both economically and spiritually. We have gained
much confidence in ourselves through directing and managing our own
affairs."

During what became to be known as the "barnstorming years" of
the Antigonish Movement, the people of eastern Nova Scotia began
to rally their spirits, pool their resources and move forward under the
guidance of Coady and his colleagues. The Extension Department never
had much money or a large staff, but its enthusiasm and dedication to

the good of ordinary people comes across clearly in Coady's speeches and writings and in the memoirs of members. The stories of successful community ventures spread, encouraging other efforts in collective action. A.B. MacDonald told how a credit union turned around life in a "bar town," where a pub bar became the credit union desk: "The story of the water turned into wine is scarcely less astonishing than the modern miracle of beer becoming butter. For the squandered cents are now savings; the bartender has been replaced by the treasurer, and the dual battle is won."

When a study club member went to jail for shooting deer out of season, A.B. sought to console him but found the man in good spirits. He greeted his visitor with a request: "Send me some pamphlets. This is a great place for a study club."

In Stellarton, Alexander Bearon, a coal miner, became an enthusiastic participant in a study club organized to start a credit union. Just before it received its charter, Beaton died in an explosion in the Allen shaft. The founders of the credit union agreed to name their self-help venture after him.

In 1932, Coady recognized that he and Father Jimmy had launched a revolution. Coady had the concept of "a world revolution" in mind, while his cousin opted for limited local action at the grassroots. Coady wondered whether "our revolutions will synchronize or not." Even while the co-ops and credit unions flourished, he kept looking beyond the mountain. In November 1938, he wrote to J.J. Harpell, a radical publisher in Quebec:

> Credit unions is only a part of our program, and probably a minor part. This alone will not solve the problem of the people.... There is still a need for readjustment of society which can only be done by an enlightened people who will create institutions in the economic and social field over which they alone have control.

Coady seemed to ignore an important aspect of the study clubs and other community ventures that he had helped to create. Working together, people in them found courage to confront the system. In one community, a politician found himself under fire:

> Somebody asked a question at a meeting which was met by the usual suave answer. Then another question. Soon it became quite evident that the whole audience was thoroughly

familiar with the question under discussion and the politician hopelessly at sea. He had to retire in confusion.

Study club members were not encouraged to engage in partisan politics. When members of the movement ran for public office in Cape Breton, they were accused of politicizing it. Coady never explained how he hoped to run a revolution without moving his people into politics. Angus L. MacDonald, the premier of Nova Scotia during the peak years of the movement, was a friend of Coady's. The priest may have talked about radical change at the world level, but contented himself with encouraging action at the community level that did not threaten politicians.

The changes that the movement brought about in the fisheries emerges in the words of Cecil Parker of Canso, who told the Extension School for Leaders in February 1935, "I am only one of those poor fishermen of Canso. I am proud, however, to be able to speak on their account." Before 1927, he and his people had been invisible: "Even our local papers very seldom had reference to the fishermen as a class." Attitudes had changed. Many of his friends "thought that Education was something a person got or did not get in his youth and that was the end of it." Now they were learning their way out of poverty. Parker then demolished another myth: "As for Organization ... everybody said you can't get the fishermen to stick together. About Co-operation we knew very little. We often heard the word used by people who had no idea what the word meant."

He described how things had changed:

We were fortunate in our friends and some of them assured us that we were never too old to learn, that the time for learning anything was when you needed it. It did not take us long to discover that this was sound doctrine and practical as far as we were concerned.

We find that our problems are fundamentally the same and if the various groups work together we shall achieve success for all groups. None of us alone can hope to solve our problems. United we stand, divided we fall.

Burden or Blessing?

> It will be difficult for the University to continue carrying the
> burden of the Extension Department.
>
> —*St. Francis Xavier University Annual Report,* 1938

Coady and his colleagues had put a small, undistinguished university in a remote part of Canada on the map. Now, because of financial
restraints, the Extension Department was seen as a "burden." Coady
had always been careful about publicizing the work of the movement,
presenting it as the result of clear thinking, hard work by his colleagues
and the efforts of local people who decided to take charge of their own
economic destinies.

While it was undervalued by the University, pilgrims came from
all over North America to find out what was happening in eastern Nova
Scotia. In 1935, King Gordon, an ardent socialist and a founding member of the Fellowship for Christian Social Order, the League for Social
Reconstruction and the Co-operative Commonwealth Federation (the
CCF, predecessor of the New Democratic Party) came to Antigonish. He
was accompanied by Peter Maniche, head of the International People's
College in Elsinore, Denmark. They travelled with an unnamed ag. rep.
who told them of Coady's work: "I tell you it's nothing short of a miracle.
And these economic changes are perhaps the least significant. It meant
that the whole of life has been raised to a higher plane."

Gordon described what he saw, catching the feel of how Coady's
people operated:

> As you enter…you are conscious of its vast sphere of influence.
> It is early morning and the secretary, who is far more than a
> secretary, is in the midst of the morning's correspondence.
> There are thirty to thirty five letters on her desk, most of them
> from study clubs and co-operative leaders.

Gordon read one of the letters. A miner wrote:

> I have been a member of No. 1 Study Club of which John
> McNab is leader. When this club started, its object was to
> develop leaders. The result is that we are all capable of lead-
> ing a club today. So I was selected three weeks ago to go and
> start a club of my own.

The study clubs had become seed beds for change, nurturing new leaders, building up their confidence, developing their native skills and talents, then expelling them to create new growth at the grassroots.

Gordon, reading through the letters, noted their common feature: "a keenness, an awareness of the conditions in the modern world." These writers had a broad perspective. And Coady's message had reached them. The letters carried "an assurance that with co-operative organization and relevant knowledge economic conditions can be vastly bettered."

He was impressed by the "literature department and the travelling library":

> There is hardly a subject in the wide field of co-operation and rural sociology and economics which is not covered by pamphlet or mimeographed material. Useful articles from current periodicals or even technical works are clipped or condensed and cut into a stencil, and then broadcast where they can be put to the most effective use.

Gordon noted the impact of the movement on communities. One had had only a single teacher:

> Now there are two very competent teachers and night school five nights a week and besides half a dozen study clubs meeting in the homes. It's marvellous. Study clubs in communities where formerly hardly a book was read, where only rarely a newspaper came in from the outside, where schools were run down and illiteracy rampant.

This visitor makes only one mention of Coady, and does not indicate that he had spoken with him. When Gordon arrived at Antigonish, 65 study club leaders were attending a course. He notes in his report, "Dr. Coady, the giant among the missionaries of the Adult Education Movement, is engaged in a lecture [at the course]."

Gordon went up to Reserve Mines, where Father Jimmy was still parish priest:

> For him the great tragedy is when an individual or a people admit defeat at the hands of their environment. For him the requisite is a great faith in the ability of the common people to regain control over their economic and spiritual destiny: the two must go together.

Alex MacIntyre, who still directed Extension's Glace Bay office, took King Gordon on a tour of credit unions and co-ops in industrial

Cape Breton. MacIntyre, described by Ida Delaney as "a born organizer and leader," had been blacklisted by the coal companies because of his involvement with union activity.

Making a meagre living as a salesman, he became an itinerant adult educator, welcomed into the homes of his friends, who asked him what they could do about their miserable living and working conditions. MacIntyre sought an alternative to the rhetoric of communist leaders in the coal fields and their belief that class warfare was the key to bettering the lives of workers. At the Diocesan Conference in Antigonish in 1932, MacIntyre spoke for two hours, telling the assembled clergy that workers were turning their backs on the Catholic Church and becoming enthralled with the ideas of communists because only they offered them any hope of a better future. In the following year Coady hired the former miner to work in industrial Cape Breton. King Gordon reported what he had achieved in two years: "He has organized something like one hundred and fifty study clubs in the district with credit unions in connection with practically every mine." MacIntyre connected study clubs to the trade union movement. The manager of the Coady Credit Union in Reserve Mines told Gordon,

> You see it is our own show.... It has made a tremendous difference to our feeling of security ... the chief effect is to be seen in the changed attitude to life and in the actual change in character: for men become different when they build up some feeling of independence which, God knows is difficult enough to do in a mining town ... [the] study clubs and credit unions are making better trade unionists.

Coady's charisma and leadership touched a wide range of people. J.D. Nelson MacDonald, who described himself as "an unorthodox clergyman," did some pioneering work improving the quality of wool in Cape Breton. Entering the United Church in 1926, he became radicalized after ministering in industrial Cape Breton. Settling in Baddeck in 1931, he attended a meeting addressed by Coady and J.C.F. MacDonnell, an ag. rep.: "I heard Dr. Coady speak many times afterwards, but he was never better than he was that night in Baddeck. He was among people whom he knew and pulled out all the stops." The Extension Department, Coady told his audience, "would teach people to learn to think, to do." He used a phrase that would become familiar, describing the Maritimes as a unit that was "large enough to be workable and small enough to be manageable." The schoolroom where the meeting was held, lit by oil lamps, could have electricity if the government harnessed the tides of the Bay of Fundy. And why could not local people turn the birch and maple trees into furniture?

In closing, Coady touched on his basic philosophy: "It is not our idea to turn men into grocers or into bankers, but rather to build the whole man – body, mind and spirit – to help men and women to look into the heart of a flower and see God."

After the priest sat down, "there was a dead silence, as if the gathering felt the presence of God in a real sense. His speech...was like a benediction." J.D. became leader of a study group, an enthusiastic co-operator, and a part-time staff member of the Extension Department.

Coady found some unlikely allies. He became active in the movement to limit the use of trawlers in offshore waters. W.H. Dennis, owner of the *Halifax Herald*, supported this cause. Appointed a senator in 1932, this conservative Nova Scotian found that the Antigonish Movement "most closely represented the political ideal for which he had groped for years." Dennis promoted Coady's work through his newspaper and radio station, CHNS. Two of his reporters, Kingsley Brown and Evelyn Tufts, covered the activities of the movement in a strongly supportive fashion. In 1938, the publisher went to meet Coady and A.B., telling them later that the editor of the Ottawa *Citizen* "would like to confer with them when next they visited Ottawa." Dennis wrote to Coady on October 6 of the same year, telling him that his movement was

> the one hopeful sign on the horizon in this part of the Dominion. I am, moreover, confident that this movement can be of incalculable benefit to the people generally. It will, of course, only reach its maximum of value if it is kept strictly free of any considerations of race or creed or politics. It is on this basis that I support this movement most cordially; and knowing your own mind in this matter, I am sure the movement will go forward along these successful lines.

The publisher involved the provincial government and the Sisters of Charity in a scheme to revitalize the fishing village of Terence Bay. He personally funded the Star of the Sea Convent, a community centre and two handicraft buildings. Dennis helped Coady and his people also, as the history of his newspaper tells:

> [Dennis] developed a personal relationship with leaders of the movement which permitted an exchange of information and ideas, as well as occasional, but timely support from him for

movement workers, clerical and lay, whose personal financial resources were meagre.

Dennis sought Coady's advice on editorial policy and news items, hosted him and A.B. at his homes in Halifax and Princeport (Cumberland County), and suggested that they approach Lord Beaverbrook and Henry Ford for money for the movement. Neither man followed up on this idea. Although Dennis was a strong supporter of Coady's work, he scolded the priest for mentioning his name in a booklet on the movement, saying, "I dislike personal publicity of this kind."

The movement's ideology and activities also led to extensive interest in the United States and to coverage that embarrassed the priest.

Bertram Fowler, In *The Lord Helps Those... How the People of Nova Scotia Are Solving Their Problems Through Co-operation*, published in 1938, began his book with these words: "There is something of a miracle in the movement that has come out of St. Francis Xavier." The jacket blurb stated, "Nowhere in the world has the co-operative movement wrought miracles comparable to those accomplished in Nova Scotia. Under the guidance of leaders connected with St. Francis Xavier University cooperation is actually transforming society."

Comparing the farmers, fishermen and miners as being "sunk in poverty as wretched as that of Southern share-croppers," the writer concluded, "A happier day has dawned for Nova Scotia." The aim of this screed, of course, was to sell the work. Fowler's book describes what is happening in eastern Nova Scotia, but does not analyze the movement.

Evelyn Tufts waxed even more euphoric. Leaving Antigonish, she noted that "a sort of radiance filled the sky, as if a hand had touched the East to light once more the star that shone when Hope was born."

Coady was well aware of the dangers of this kind of writing: "We are a little fearful here of the effects of over-publicizing the Antigonish Movement. The cause has already been hurt by many writers who overstated the achievements of the movement and did not interpret it properly."

In 1938, A.B. MacDonald threatened to quit if he did not receive a salary increase. Somehow, Coady found the money. That same year, St. F.X. described the Extension Department as a burden. Meanwhile, Cardinal Eugenio Pacelli sent a message commending its work: "Social life has a sacredness of its own when imbued with the spirit of the gospel and based on charity and justice." Pacelli, who became Pope Pius XII the next year, praised Coady and his staff "who had dedicated themselves and their all to the betterment of the Christian people."

The Extension's conference in August 1939 drew people from 28 American states and 40 students and professors from Columbia University in New York. Extension staff had helped to set up fisheries co-ops in British Columbia, and A.B. was invited to Manitoba to tell people there about the movement.

But Coady's vision of the good society transcended all the local efforts. He began to become discontented and to write and talk about the shortcomings of his followers.

5

Coady and the Great Default

Ah, but a man's reach should exceed his grasp,
Or what's a heaven for?
                    —Robert Browning, "Andrea del Sarto"

B y the time the only book that Moses Coady ever wrote, *Masters of
Their Own Destiny*, appeared in 1939, the author and his colleagues
had every reason to be proud of what they had achieved. In less
than ten years, with meagre resources, they had transformed the lives
of thousands of poor people, educated a new generation of leaders, and
brought hope to a people once lost in despair and inertia. On a visit to
the University of Alberta in 1927, Father Jimmy Tompkins had admired
a big map in the U of A Extension Department. Coloured pins showed
the locations served by the department; they were sprinkled from the
Montana border to the Peace River country. Visitors to Coady's office
were shown a similar map of the Maritimes. Scores of coloured pins
identified different kinds of co-operative ventures in the region. They
were thick in eastern Nova Scotia, Halifax, Prince Edward Island, Saint
John, Moncton and along the coast of New Brunswick.

Despite these achievements, Coady remained discontented. His
reach still exceeded his grasp, and the heaven he had envisaged for the
ordinary people of the region had not yet come into being. Malcolm
MacLellan, the priest's friend and biographer, recognized his contradic-

tory nature, his belief in the potential of every human being and his impatience with human fallibility:

> Dr. Coady's philosophy produced three important results: it created a sense of togetherness; it promoted a concrete program of study and action; and it fostered mutual help and brotherhood. He was the idealist who envisioned greatness and a better way of life, and the realist who came to grips with the everyday problems of people and proposed practical solutions. Thus he could synthesize seeming opposites or apparent contradictions, and reconcile a radicalism reaching to the grassroots of society with a conservatism rooted in traditional principles.

All social movements begin with individuals, voices in the wilderness, proclaiming that a new world awaits those who will work towards bringing it into being. Charismatic individuals – and Coady was certainly one – draw around them a band of faithful followers who spread his or her message. As more and more people join the movement, its activities became less diffuse and more organized, focusing on day-to-day matters, maintaining things, paying less attention to its original vision and the mission it created. Sometimes a lucky chance or a shift in society or a force outside this community of believers benefits its members. Coady referred to "the lobster, one of the homeliest of fishes, [that] proved to be the economic liberator of our people, and it may be the cultural and spiritual liberator also." Lobster, once the food of the poor in the Maritimes, became a delicacy in the 1930s. Locally owned canneries added value to the crustacean, and the government subsidized a vessel that took fresh ones to market. Only a leader with Coady's vision and imagination could connect the humble lobster with cultural development in communities.

Coady believed, as did his cousin Father Jimmy, that "Ideas are more powerful than bullets. They will wreck or build great empires, economic and political, more effectively than the best war material invented." As the movement progressed and more co-operative ventures came into being, Coady began to see it as more than a form of economic guerilla warfare. His idea of a utopian society had to contend with people's practical needs and selfish demands as ordinary folk gained more control over their own lives. Coady believed that his nephew Leo, son of Joe and Katie, had leadership potential. He wrote to him:

Be good and sensible. I do not mean old-fashioned or dour, but full of enthusiasm that comes from a vision of great things to be done. The world can be tremendously interesting to a man who has the vision and moral fibre to discipline himself in preparation for a great career.

The Antigonish Movement skimmed off the best and the brightest people in the region, who saw in it opportunities for creating new lives for themselves and others. In *Knowledge for the People*, Father Jimmy called for

A handful of devoted men prepared to make this work their single interest, and to consecrate to it their whole time and energies for no compensation beyond daily bread if necessary. And just because their arduous [task], so exacting (and full, it may be said, of disappointment and discouragement), must be its own reward, these men cannot normally be drawn from the laity.

The priests in the region served as anchors for the movement, but they could not wander the highways and byways preaching the gospel of adult education, as Father Jimmy envisaged. And while many young men and women found fulfillment working with Coady and his colleagues, they did not have the passionate commitment to social justice that kept the pioneers going. They found careers in the credit unions and co-ops, settled down and lived as normally as their neighbours. They began to pay less and less attention to the need for ongoing education, and these programs gradually fell into abeyance. The Maritimes lacked a large pool of bright, able and ambitious people who would dedicate their lives to the welfare of others and bring into being the new world that Coady envisaged.

As the years went by, Coady began to increasingly resemble his irascible cousin, Father Jimmy. Although kindly men, both had harsh edges to their tongues and could lay on the rawhide whip if they saw human failure. Their speeches often sounded like the pronouncements of Old Testament prophets who called for a change of heart among the faithless.

Coady told his audiences about three Patagonians – the 1930s equivalent of visitors from outer space – who came to Nova Scotia. They behaved politely, but wondered what kind of people lived there. Surrounded by magnificent forests, they lived in homes that were little better than shacks. The land could grow an abundance of food, yet they were ill-nourished. Unemployment was rampant – but there was plenty of work to be done.

Coady's belief in the power of ideas to change the hearts and actions of men and women came up against powerful forces that kept people in dependency and insecurity. He never mentions the petty, patronage-ridden political system in Nova Scotia in the 1930s. The forestry sector, which Coady saw as a source of jobs and fine wooden products, was dominated by absentee owners and inefficient local operators. Here, as elsewhere, corruption ran rampant. C.W. Anderson, a Liberal Member of the Legislative Assembly, cut wood illegally on crown land in Guysborough County. Another "big man," Albert Parsons, a Conservative MLA, also looted the forests – and failed to pay his taxes. John Bigelow, a forester, sought the help of the Extension Department in breaking the grip of the middlemen who exploited pulpwood producers. Working for the Department of Agriculture – many farmers cut wood on their own land – Bigelow developed lasting and cordial relationships with Coady and his colleagues. He began to organize pulpwood co-ops, beginning in Richmond County in Cape Breton. In the post-war years, Bigelow encountered hostility from woodlot owners and lumbermen because of their fear of socialism. A minister of agriculture cautioned him against getting too close to the promoters of co-ops at St. F.X.

A study of the forest industry in Nova Scotia points up Coady's great fault – his unwillingness or inability to confront a corrupt political system – as well as indicating his achievements in organizing poor and marginalized rural people. The authors point out the problems of bringing rational management practices and economic democracy to a backward province: "Common to all social strata was a political and economic culture premised on partisanship, clientism, and crude material exploitation." In a paper published in 1997, James Sacouman, a Marxist sociologist, claimed that the Antigonish Movement undercut militant trade unionism and socialism in the region, and created a class of small-time bourgeoisie. Coady believed he could fashion an ideal society without engaging in partisan politics, while a small clique of politicians and big business people maintained a firm grip on power. If workers in the steel and coal industries went on strike when wages were cut, the government sent in the army.

Coady also had to contend with trends in international politics that affected his church. The tensions in the Catholic Church between autocracy and democracy had come to a head at the Rural and Industrial Conference in 1937. Tour members from the Co-operative League of the U.S.A. were told that Coady "had developed and directed one of the most practical and interesting co-operative ventures in North America." The visitors admired co-op creameries, fishing ventures and other self-help activities as they moved around eastern Nova Scotia, boosting the morale of the members.

The conference heard from Father Alex MacKenzie, who had just returned from Italy. He described Mussolini, the Italian dictator, as "the man of the hour." The Catholic Church looked to strong leaders to restore order in Europe. Newsreel footage from this time shows nuns in trucks passing in parade before Mussolini, arms lifted in the fascist salute. During the Spanish Civil War, the Catholic Church backed Francisco Franco, who became the national dictator, against the democratically elected government that took power in 1936. The republicans murdered many nuns and priests after the war broke out, and in turn were murdered by the fascists.

The 1937 conference passed a resolution opposing Fascism, National Socialism, and all other such forms of dictatorship. It asserted that the philosophy and principles of the co-operative movement were "diametrically opposed to any order that would limit the freedom and therefore the activities and growth of all individuals."

As a democrat with an ecumenical outlook who strove to keep partisan politics out of his movement, Coady had to defend it against charges that it was promoting Catholicism and communism, although after the 1937 conference, he heard that Protestants had been responsible for the motion condemning fascism.

Coady's health was beginning to deteriorate at this time. In 1936, he had been sick for six weeks before setting off to tour New Brunswick. Some of his cherished projects failed to come to fruition in the years after this. The Rural and Industrial Conference in 1937 urged the government to deal with unemployment by settling "rural-minded young men" in farms. Father Michael Gillis was behind this scheme. A rural romantic like Coady, Gillis saw the good life arising from close contact with the land and the creation of self-reliant individuals and communities. In 1938, Coady admitted to a friend that the settlement scheme had largely failed and that few young people had returned to the land. He continued to defend the movement against the claim that it was creating a peasant economy in eastern Nova Scotia, turning back the clock at a time when urbanization, industrialization and rural migration were accelerating.

As the Extension Department expanded its operations in industrial Cape Breton, new tensions emerged. From its outpost in Glace Bay,

Ida Gallant and Alex MacIntyre wrote to Coady in 1938 about some of their concerns. At that time, the Extension Department had eight full-time members, seven part-time field workers, and support staff. Gallant and MacIntyre, two hard workers, claimed that their resources were being stretched thin. Many of the staff had originally been chairs of study clubs. They spent their time supervising and advising existing credit unions and study clubs, rather than encouraging the formation of new ones. The study clubs themselves suffered from indifferent, argumentative and dictatorial leaders; the meetings were poorly organized, poorly attended, lacked focus and merely became places for swapping gossip. They needed "personal attention and the supervision of some responsible person in the community." The Extension Department also lacked reading material for ordinary people. Readers in industrial Cape Breton told Gallant that *The Extension Bulletin* "is not written for the average man." McIntyre claimed that the successes of the movement had been overemphasized and that too much publicity had been given to the achievements in small communities like Little Dover. Bertram Fowler's book *The Lord Helps Those...* called Coady "the man of the hour [with] the ability, through his understanding of people, to arouse them to thoughts of action. He could persuade logically while he put new dynamic force into his listeners." But Coady's logic still did not lead him to confront the political system.

Gregory Baum, who spoke with old-timers in Cape Breton, concluded that the Labour College, an early idea of Father Jimmy's that the Extension Department had organized in Cape Breton, had helped workers to "gain greater self-confidence, but...it had no definable influence on the labour movement." Workers associated the activities of the Extension Department with co-op and credit union formation; Baum concluded that the department "had no direct influence on political development."

While the movement did not confront politicians, its example was certainly noted. In 1940, Clarence Gillis, a tough ex-soldier active in the co-op and credit union movement, took a House of Commons seat for the Co-operative Commonwealth Federation (CCF) in Cape Breton. In that year, he wrote in *The New Commonwealth*, the party's paper, that miners, under the guidance of the Extension Department, "are practically taking over the economic resources of the province." Gillis, in his first speech in the House, on June 4, 1940, dwelled on unemployment, claiming,

> The people of Nova Scotia are making a wonderful effort to solve their own economic problems by co-operative action.

They have already established 180 credit unions, 43 stores, 17 lobster factories, 7 fish plants, 8 community industries and some 10 other co-operatives. The total number of co-operative organizations in the Maritimes is 442.

Telling the Story

Always more at home as a speaker than a writer, he found it difficult to organize and articulate his ideas in a book.

—Malcom MacLellan, *Coady Remembered*

Coady grew up in a rural area with a strong oral tradition. Although widely read, he had difficulty with the written word. He had lots of ideas, but found it hard to express them clearly on paper. As Laidlaw put it, "In writing he tended to be heavy and pedantic, but in speech he was breezy, witty and given to more picturesque language than he put on paper."

In 1937, the Rockefeller Foundation gave Coady a grant to write a book on the movement. There was a great need for such a work, as the achievements of the movement became more widely known, and often misrepresented. Coady struggled with the book, which he saw as a way of outlining the blueprint for the good and abundant society that he had striven to bring into being, for two years before it was finished. *Masters* flashes with some of the vigorous images that marked the author's speeches:

When we were boys, they used to send us out cutting alders when there was nothing else to do on the farm. Before leaving for the woods, we'd get our axes so sharp you could shave a sleeping mouse with them without waking it up.

He always carried a small black notebook in which he jotted down his "nuggets": "A brand new idea popped into my mind when I woke in the middle of the night and I reached for my little book."

After thinking through his ideas for a few days, he would arrive at his office, beaming and triumphant: "I've got it ... the biggest idea I ever had in my life!" Coady would then dictate this particular finding to a secretary. After revising the text, he would show it to his staff, asking them, "What do you think of that? I think it's a corker."

Ellen Arsenault became his secretary in 1947. He selected her because she had worked for a bank as well as being a teacher. Coady would phone her at seven in the morning. "Would you take this down? I don't want to lose this idea," he would say. Arsenault would frantically try to keep up with her boss as he chatted away for ten minutes. When she arrived at the office at nine, Coady would greet her, saying, "Have you got my notes with you? Well, don't bother to type them now. Just listen for a minute. I want to clarify the ideas in my mind before we get down to work." He would then go over the same ideas he had dictated over the phone. As MacLellan put it, "Literary gems were to be grasped and recorded before they would disappear like shining bubbles dissolved in the fury of a stormy sea." Arsenault typed the notes and the dictation, and Coady went over them until he was satisfied that he had caught the idea on paper.

He tackled the writing of *Masters* in the same way, but realized he needed help. Zita O'Hearn, whom he had just hired, helped him focus his ideas and develop a coherent theme for the book.

Speaking engagements and short courses kept Coady busy until the end of 1937. The Rockefeller Foundation suggested that he travel to a retreat they owned in Beaufort, South Carolina, to work on the book. After speaking in Boston in late February, Coady headed to the retreat, and O'Hearn began to work with him on the book on "our Adult Education program."

She reported that he "was no more anxious to get down to work than he had been at home. He missed his supporting audiences and his health was failing. I did not realize how much until, on our way in April, he had to enter a hospital in Boston." At the age of 56, Mighty Moses had begun to falter, and from then on he became increasingly concerned about his health.

Back in Antigonish, in a familiar setting and with the help of O'Hearn and others, Coady completed his manuscript in May 1939, with a lot of help from the staff.

Coady was tense. Usually gregarious, he dealt curtly with Dr. H.P. MacPherson, the former rector of the University, when he dropped into the office for a chat. After a weekend of work in May, A.B. drove Coady to his plane at Halifax airport for the flight to New York.

He delivered the manuscript to Harper and Brothers publishers, and then was admitted to hospital as his health began to fail. From there, he worked with editors who found the book too large and unwieldy. They cut the text in half, and subtitled the book "The Story of the Antigonish Movement of Adult Education Through Economic Cooperation" to reach the widest possible readership. As Zita O'Hearn put it, "Here at last was the answer for the doubters, the pharisees, and the sincerely concerned friends who could not help wondering if perhaps the men of

X were not going too far with the realm of 'dirty economics,' straying from the paths of mind and spirit."

This remark goes to the core of many of Coady's concerns. His vision of a new society rested on the creation of an alternative form of economic development, created by ordinary people through their own efforts. Conflict, class warfare, economic injustice and oppression would vanish if people learned to work together for the common good. These ideas are as pertinent today as they were when *Masters* was published over 60 years ago.

Weeks after the book was released, the Second World War broke out when the Germans invaded Poland on September 1, 1939. Canada declared war nine days later. Over the next six years, as the opposing forces mobilized huge numbers of men and enormous quantities of material, the command and control model of leadership re-emerged as the key to success.

The Book

> To all those unnamed noble souls who without remuneration
> are working overtime in the cause of humanity.
>
> —Dedication, *Masters of Their Own Destiny*

Coady's book carried the imprimatur of the archbishop of Antigonish, and the *Nihil obstat* of the Censor Deputatus, H.P. MacPherson. (These stamps of approval indicated that the work was doctrinally sound, as far as the Catholic Church was concerned.) Coady discusses themes he had presented over the years in his addresses and short articles. He tells nothing about himself: how his upbringing in the Margaree influenced his work, what motivated him to engage in social and economic action to free the poor from oppression. He credits others with the success of the movement, as his fine dedication indicates. At St. F.X., he says, "Ideas were not only generated and sifted, but a body of able men were being themselves educated and were learning to think and work together. This collaboration among leaders was the very life blood when [the movement] got under way."

Mass meetings opened the minds of people, and the study clubs generated "one of the glories of the movement" – new leaders. Coady wrote that his approach to adult education was "founded on the idea that the learner is most important in the education process. The educator must take men and groups of men where he finds them, and work with their background, interests and capabilities."

The movement began with the failure of the formal education system to meet the needs of ordinary people. Coady plays down the tensions that pervaded St. F.X. and the Maritimes during the 1920s as "the Bolsheviks of a better sort" tried to make the university responsive to the needs of local communities. He pays tribute to H.P. MacPherson ("the old Rector"), Father Jimmy, "Little Doc" Hugh MacPherson, Fathers Miles Tompkins and Michael Gillis, and other members of the small band of pioneer activists. Then he mentions the twelve farmers who attended the study group he organized in the Margaree in 1927–28.

"The Antigonish Movement was founded on the idea that if the work could be universalized, great good would be done," he writes. Coady identifies three "distinguishing characteristics" of the movement:

1)   the small study club;

2)   discussion issuing in economic group action; and

3)   the willingness of the more intelligent members of the group to place their abilities at the disposal of the slower members.

After telling of Father Jimmy's work in Canso, and dealing with his own organizing work among the fishermen, the author states:

The idea of launching out into this movement was new and, in those days, revolutionary. St. F.X. had little money. A program such as was contemplated would naturally raise Opposition. The question of how the people would respond…was yet in doubt. It took courage to face the issue.

Coady describes the beauty of the Maritimes, which he saw as "perhaps the great social laboratory" where new ideas about adult education and economic development could be identified and tested. He breaks into poetry to describe this "Divine mosaic by a Master hand" before turning to one of his obsessions, "The Great Default of the People": "We have begun our program of adult education and economic co-operation by dealing with human problems, and we have said frankly to people that their situation is due mainly to their own default."

If the people lived in poverty and dependency, then it was their own fault – not because they didn't work hard, but because they didn't work together. Coady pictures coal miners coming home from work, washing themselves and calling it a day; fishermen thinking they had done enough when they landed their daily catches; farmers knocking off after a day of drudgery. Instead of relaxing, "the people must put in extra work on a program of study and enlightenment [to] create the institutions that will enable them to obtain control of the instruments" and create "the new society." Coady assumed that everyone had the same stamina, energy and commitment he possessed as he tried to lead them into a utopian society where everyone co-operated.

Coady used an image that he had cited many times to describe how people could create this new society. He compared the economy to a tottering smokestack that had to be replaced by a "strong, upright chimney." The builders of the smokestack had been careless in laying the foundation, allowing it to get out of plumb. When the stack reached 30 feet, "it tilts a little, but is still firm and the building continues."

By the time the smokestack reaches its full height "it has become a dizzily leaning tower." Even the builder fears his creation. He hastens to prop it up, using guy wires to ensure that the stack will not collapse. Coady notes that there "is now less danger of a catastrophe but the structure is by no means safe." No one can repair it. The smokestack must be rebuilt. In the same way, the economy had been badly built, and now had to be propped up. The Antigonish Movement's smokestack would be built solidly from the ground up, by people creating credit unions and co-ops. The first step in the process came through mass meetings and the people's determination to rebuild themselves and society. To do this required "scientific thinking." Coady always thought in terms of blueprints and formulae.

Masters devotes a chapter to "The Spread of Adult Education," citing E.L. Thorndike's book *Adult Learning*, which "gave scientific confirmation of the Antigonish theory of adult learning." Then Coady tells of Larry's River, Havre Boucher, Little Dover and other communities, naming the priests who anchored the movement there. He makes special mention of J.D. Nelson MacDonald. The work with farmers and in the industrial areas, and the spread of credit unions throughout the Maritimes and western Canada are described, and a page devoted to study clubs for women and their involvement in handicrafts.

In 1938, Alex MacIntyre had written to Coady, suggesting that too much attention was being paid to criticizing the exploiters of the people of Nova Scotia. Coady describes what happened when co-operators chartered a ship and imported flour and feed from Ontario: "This precipitated a struggle. Vested interests all over the country resorted to every known means to meet the new competition." Coady's work encouraged people to come together to offer an alternative to so-called private enterprise. Rather than lamenting the ills of capitalism, union organizers had begun to beat its proponents at their own game!

The book also deals with one of the most important aspects of the movement. Of the short courses for local leaders, the author states: "Nothing in our whole technique ever turned out more successfully than this school." He explains the results of this approach to adult education:

> The field of social theory was opened up to these men and women in a simple way; the instruments that would give the people an opportunity to realize their dreams were outlined; the technique of study and discussion groups was actually demonstrated.

After a month of this kind of learning, the participants "went forth with a flair for work that rivals the best zeal of the Communists." Coady mentions a problem that Ida Gallant had brought to his attention: "The most difficult phase of the adult education movement is the preparation of interesting material for the study group." He pays tribute to "the sympathetic attitude of the Department of Fisheries," which funded the work of the Extension Department, then returns to another of his visions for his people: "We start with the simple material things that are vital to human living and move on up the scale to the more cultural and refining activities that make life whole and complete." By 1939, some of this dream had been realized. Drama clubs, debating societies, choral groups, and orchestras had emerged from study clubs.

The book then discusses a topic still of concern in our own time: the buying power of consumers and their ability to influence the economy. To Coady, each purchase at a co-op was a small hammer blow against the exploitive system controlled by local merchants. A chapter in *Masters* mentions "social entrepreneurs," innovative individuals working for the common good who had brought into being consumer co-ops, the co-op housing scheme in Tompkinsville, and a co-op health insurance program in Antigonish. Such people had something in common with entrepreneurs in the private sector who were decent chaps: they were producers, blazing new trails and creating wealth.

Coady criticizes unions because they simply fought corporations over wages and conditions of work, rather than encouraging their members to use consumer power: "Each little worker has an economic hose through which he sprays his earnings." But they pointed their hoses in the wrong direction. The lawns of those who provided goods and services "are green and their flowers are fresh while the worker's own yard is an ash-heap." Through co-operative action, the "little worker" could spray his own lawn and put the surplus "into reservoirs for the dry season." Credit unions had become a powerful tool for consumers, although when the idea was first introduced, "the fear was often expressed that somebody would run away with the money." Coady then turns his attention to the sloppy way in which farmers, fishermen and other producers handled their crops and catches: "It is almost impossible for small, independent farmers or fishermen to produce a commodity in sufficient volume and of uniform quality in any scheme of individual marketing." The pioneers of rural revitalization in eastern Nova Scotia, with the help of government, had encouraged primary producers to improve the quality of wool, grain, lobsters and other cash crops and to market them collectively. Some farmers taunted their neighbours, claiming they were making more money than those in co-ops. Co-op marketing was successful although fishermen and farmers still clung to their individualism even as they struggled to survive. Coady cites the Antigonish turkey co-operative, the collective marketing of pulpwood in West Arichat and Louisdale, a milk pasteurization plant owned by farmers in Sydney, and examples of fish and lobster sales by groups to indicate what producers can do when they pool their efforts.

Coady devotes the last third of the book to the philosophy that underpinned his work. It was based on the idea that "the full life is the gradual realization of human potentialities." Adult education could create balanced lives for people: "A three-legged stool that has one leg shorter than the others is of little value and less beauty. An unbalanced man is no more desirable." He caught the lure of his movement as it created balanced individuals through economic co-operation: "The thrill of achievement that comes from operating new and successful enterprises in the material and economic fields exhilarates [adult learners]." To motivate people, adult educators must first satisfy them: "Start where you are, concentrate on what interests people, but also provide them with a vision of a better future." This sentence sums up Coady's approach to learning. Once people had some economic security they could move on to higher things:

> From the people, raised to new levels, will arise poets, painters and musicians to give expression to the new and eternal truths that beat within our breasts. As in nature, so in man, the lofty mountains shall not rise from the level plains but from the foothills.

Coady's discontent with the present economic system arose from his memories of the self-sufficient life in the Margaree: "If a man wanted cabbages or potatoes, he grew them himself." There was "an almost infinite capacity to produce, but a definite inability to distribute because so many must profit by the process." Co-operators could condition people "to the point where they are able to manipulate effectively the other forces that should operate in a democratic society." For him, co-operation was not about being paid more for less and buying sugar for a lower price. It was about building democracy: "A few hundred thousand rugged individuals have robbed the rest of us of our individualism. Along with this, the mechanization of industry has deprived people of any opportunity for self-expression or personal initiative."

Coady scrutinized the political scene, noting that the "tendency is for candidates to represent the interests that put them in power." Co-ops had to be politically neutral, but their members need not be, for they were learning "intelligent political action" as they worked for the common good. He favoured public ownership of utilities such as electricity, even if private business cried "Socialism!" at "the mere mention of state ownership." Business had to be kept in check: "In the past competition was expected to do this, but competition is dead and economic dictatorship has taken its place."

The book discusses "The Confusion of Tongues": "From the radio, the pulpit and the press, come much good counsel and many vague generalizations. The world is literally cluttered up with suggestions and the common people are confused and confounded by them."

Abstract plans had little appeal for people if they could not undertake them: "If people cannot do the things advocated, then some sort of dictatorship must do them."

The Marxist belief in proletarian revolution came under attack with one of Coady's striking images:

> Revolutionary Socialism, or Communism, takes for granted that man in his social evolution can skip intermediaries.... Man is limited in his own nature and the nature of his surroundings, and cannot make things happen any faster than nature will permit. The chicken cannot be hatched any faster by putting two hens on the nest.

Coady had no illusions about the challenges still facing the movement:

We are still rolling the huge stone up the steep hill. If at any point in the ascent we take off the pressure it will go crashing to the bottom. Before we can be sure of ourselves we have to get it firmly at rest on the plateau above.

His book swoops and dives, using simple images and examples to make his points. People must "find their own lobster." He then cites the Scholastics – "the end is the first in intention and the last in execution" – before moving on to a discussion of the ideas of Plato and Aristotle. Throughout the book are short, pithy sayings that capture a wealth of knowledge in a few words: "Thinking is difficult." "Culture is growth of personality." "The teacher who refuses to criticize conditions as they exist invites suspicion."

His ecumenical perspective on local development echoes the insistence of the Rochdale pioneers that co-ops had to be "neutral in the matter of religion":

We cannot speak of Catholic co-operation or Protestant co-operation, of Buddhist, Mohammedan, Shinto, or Hebrew economics any more than we can speak of Quaker chemistry or Mormon mathematics. Truth is non-denominational and at the disposal of all.

However, he stressed that co-operation needs religion and religion needs co-operation:

The religiously minded man will use all the good things of God's creation to further the cause of humanity and to insure the salvation of souls. He will stop talking about putting religion into co-operatives and begin putting religion into co-operators.

Coady's profound spirituality infuses the book as he scolds his readers for inaction: "We cannot ask Almighty God to perform miracles of grace while we ignore the natural means now at our disposal for affecting a change." *Masters* promotes the concept of the organic community beloved of Catholic theologians seeking stability in times of rapid change. Coady ties the idea to those golden days of his early life in the Margaree and a time of harmony among humans:

If we changed [society] from an aggregation of fighting individualists to an integrated body of co-ordinated and co-operative cells, every individual person could then be a better, more useful, and more serviceable member of the organic whole.

Each could then really give according to his abilities where he received according to his needs.

While much of what Coady writes has relevance to our time, his picture of the ideal society conjures up the image of a beehive, with everyone working together for the good of the whole in an orderly and organized manner. He had little time for charity, which he felt did nothing for human dignity and did not give people "a chance to make their own contribution and to move under their own power." Co-operative action enabled needy people "to contribute to the general good and the greater glory of God." Coady had great faith in the human capacity "to recuperate – find the strength to rise, straighten up, throw back [a] noble head, and gaze into the sun."

Coady's poetical impulses paralleled his practical approach to the task of creating a just and compassionate society through "the power of newly released group energies." Attempts to do this had to contend with "active opposition from the vested interests, passive resistance from the masses." The former had replaced "invested lords and nobles. We, the people, have had the ball and chain removed from one foot only." He admits that the Antigonish Movement had its failures, but does not give examples. He knew with certainty that economic democracy would lead to political democracy and so change the world:

> An ignorant man may win a sweepstake. He may not and will not win laurels as a co-operator. Being a co-operator implies learning, the learning of new techniques; and no man can learn a new technique without suffering a period of temporary inefficiency. Therein lies the kernel of a valuable bit of philosophy.

Always dreaming beyond the mountains that hemmed in the imaginations of others, Coady describes how he came up with a grand scheme for economic development through local schemes for adult education that could embody the best of European schemes. He expressed the hope that regional study groups would create autonomous learning institutions that would link up with "any university or agency that is willing and competent to help them." He remains realistic regarding what academics could offer ordinary people:

> However much progressive professors may desire to participate in the invigorating exercise of directing alert adults in building a nation, they must continue to perform their more respectable and less offensive functions.

If they so desire, he writes, communities could establish their own learning centres: "All that is needed in the beginning is a director, an office and a stenographer." And he describes the vision of a "people's research institution, owned and financed by people themselves and operated for the benefit of the entire country" – an idea that never came to fruition.

On the last page of the book, Coady's soaring imagination addresses the task of "Creating great and good men":

> We have no desire to remain at the beginning, to create a nation of mere shopkeepers, whose thoughts run only to groceries and dividends. We want our men to look into the sun and into the depths of the sea. We want them to explore the hearts of flowers and the hearts of fellow-men. We want them to live, to love, to play and pray with all their being. We want them to be men, whole men, eager to explore all the avenues of life and to attain perfection in all their faculties. We want for them to enjoy all that a generous God and creative men have placed at their disposal. We desire above all that they will discover and develop their own capacities for creation. It is good to appreciate; it is godlike to create.

The way into the future, as Coady saw it, lay in a return to the past, to that land of lost content of his boyhood when people submerged their individualism in the quest for the common good, and strengthened their unique capabilities and potential for becoming better human beings.

War clouds already loomed over Europe as Coady worked on his manuscript, and he made a plea for peace:

> Men...were not born to hate but to love ... we are victims of a vicious system bred by greed and nurtured by the will to power.... Man was not made for bestial fighting. Man was conceived in peace. And in peace he shall find his lost virtues and his departed joys.

Adult educators and co-operators welcomed *Masters*: one review, headed "What a Tale it Is!", captures the essence of this inspirational work.

Coady lived for another 20 years after the publication of his book, through times that made his vision of a co-operative society more and more difficult to achieve. He planned to write an autobiography after the war, but never completed it. He left the notes for it with his secretary, Ellen Arsenault. He continued to talk and to write, however; his scattered works were collected by Alex Laidlaw in *The Man from Margaree,* published in 1971.

In the post-war years, his restless mind continued to have problems articulating his ideas on paper. In 1948, he sent a copy of a letter to Father Jimmy to a civil servant in Ottawa, apologizing for the text: "It was dictated at the end of the day in a hurry and right to the machine – when I started a sentence there is no way of correcting an error and I was twisting it around as best I could."

Coady, although a man of action, was a procrastinator, one of the many paradoxes of this extraordinary Canadian. Ellen Arsenault recalled how he took an hour to write a letter to the widow of a friend: "Dear Mrs. M., It was a great shock for me to learn – no, change that, the poor woman isn't interested in my grief," and so forth. When the letter was finished, he showed it to Laidlaw: "I want you to see the letter that Ellen and I wrote." As his secretary noted, "Such lavish giving of credit when no credit was due was characteristic of him until the day he died."

After the end of the Second World War, Coady became recognized as a world leader in adult education and co-operation. He retained his humanity and humility even as the movement he had led began to lose the original vision and to become more concerned with bottom-line matters than with the human spirit. Forces that had been latent during the golden years of the movement emerged and began to change the lives of people in eastern Nova Scotia, undercutting the work he had done to bring into being the good and abundant society.

But still, he persevered in his appointed task of making a better world for the people he had served so well through his unique organizing and visionary abilities.

6

The Movement and the Mover

> With individual persons and in specific cases, Coady was
> a compassionate man, but feelings of compassion did not
> occupy him for long because the focus of his mind shifted
> quickly from individuals to humanity in the mass, to human
> beings collectively.
>
> —Alexander Laidlaw, *The Man from Margaree*

The years between 1939, when his book appeared, and 1952, when Coady retired as Director of Extension, proved difficult ones for the co-operative movement. During this time, however, the man from Margaree rose to international prominence. Scores of individuals from all walks of life came to Antigonish to study the movement and to seek his advice. While spreading his message of hope for the future, he became increasingly pessimistic about what he heard and learned on his travels in North America and Europe, although he kept his vision of a better world through co-operation alive.

For health reasons, he changed some of his personal habits. Alex Laidlaw, who replaced A.B. MacDonald as assistant director of the Extension Department in 1944, recalled Coady's energy:

> If you worked with him, the first thing you would feel was
> that his mind never rested: he was always in a hurry, always
> going places, always doing things. He rose early and had half

a day's work done by 9:00 o'clock in the morning. He was a man of great self-discipline. When some of his habits were found to be bad, he said: "OK, that's the end of it." At one time, he smoked heavily. [In 1942] his doctor told him smoking was bad for him. He said: "OK, I'm through." At one time he drank too much. Then he made up his mind: "That's the end of it" – and he never touched alcohol again. When anything interfered with his health or his work, he would exert whatever discipline was necessary.

Coady was "almost fanatical on the question of food" and believed that bad nutrition took the courage out of people: "Feed people for two generations on white bread and white sugar and such stuff, and a dictator can do what he pleases with them – they have no vitality ... they can't fight back."

He started every day with the simple Latin phrase: *In Nomine Domine* [In the Name of the Lord]. His staff recall the energy and openness of the man who treated them as his equals. When the Vatican elevated Coady to the rank of Monsignor in 1946, he burst out: "The sons of bitches! They can't do that to me." He felt that the honour would separate him, elevate him above the people he sought to serve. But at the same time he enjoyed wearing a monsignor's vestments, and friends joked about the possibilities of Coady acquiring a cardinal's hat.

His national and international fame did not affect him. As Laidlaw put it,

> There is the memory of the humble, always destitute priest who, in the days when he was making headlines, received money gifts galore and who couldn't get rid of them fast enough. God alone knows how many boats, nets and babies he financed. A Protestant admirer operating a clothing store provided most of what he wore, the University fed and housed him, the people who took him half-way around the world for speaking engagements paid his expenses. "What do I need money for, boy?" he asked this writer when it was suggested he hold on to something.

Coady, with his ideas about service to others and his memory of his days in the Margaree and the ideal organic society, confronted new challenges during the war as governments intruded more and more into the co-operative field.

In January 1942, J.H. Michaud, the federal Minister of Fisheries, informed Coady that he had written to Father J.L. Chiasson of Shippegan, New Brunswick, who was a member of the Extension Department, to complain that co-operators in Gloucester County were handing over control of lobster canning to a private company, and that a firm from Portland, Maine, was acquiring control of the marketing of processed fish. "They get all the work done by the co-operators and derive the benefits," he wrote. He believed all catches should be sold through United Maritime Fishermen. The co-operative society had encountered local realities. Chiasson wrote back to the minister, pointing out that this was a perpetual problem for small co-operatives. Those in his area were undercapitalized and lacked modern equipment. They had lost money in the previous lobster season, so they decided to sell their catches to a private company that had access to markets in the United States. The priest noted that UMF was, nevertheless, playing a larger role in the fisheries of New Brunswick by marketing smelts and engaging in other activities that benefited its members.

At its annual meeting in 1943, UMF set up a Reconstruction Committee and asked Coady to chair it. Its brief defended the inshore fishery as a major source of employment, asked for a floor under fish prices (this had been done for agricultural products), urged the government to set up a chain of freezers and cold storage facilities to be run as a public utility, and opposed the operations of trawlers and draggers.

Coady felt for the small-boat fishermen of the region, and made enormous efforts to support their efforts at making a living. But they frustrated him in many ways. When Laidlaw drove with the priest to a fishing village on a fine, crisp day, they expected to see all the boats out fishing. Instead, the fishermen had tied up their boats at the dock, and were sitting around talking or doing light chores. They greeted Coady "in a mixed attitude of friendliness and worship."

"Why aren't you fishing today?" he asked impatiently.

"We haven't any bait," they replied.

"And why haven't you any bait?" Coady snapped back. He continued to ask more questions. The lack of bait "lay not in some adverse fate or indifferent government officials, but in themselves." Then Coady laid on the rawhide whip:

> If you had done in the past ten or 20 years what you could have done and should have done, and if your fathers and grandfathers had done the same, there would be no scarcity of bait and you'd be out fishing today where you should be!

Inshore fishermen had developed their own culture. They wanted some degree of freedom in their lives: they had an inherent distrust of governments and had not learned how to influence their decisions. Coady was caught between the rock of the individualistic ways of fishermen and the hard place that came with increasing government intervention in the fisheries. The federal government paid no heed to the brief from UMF's Reconstruction Committee. Dr. Stewart Bates, a Harvard economics graduate who was to become Deputy Minister of Fisheries in 1947, produced another report in 1944 pointing out that the Atlantic fishery was "undercapitalized, inefficient, and lacking in technology that could raise productivity."

Was the fishery to be an economic business activity to generate profits, or a way of life to sustain people and their small communities? The tensions between these two views continues to pervade our time. There was little that Coady, for all his charismatic presence, energy, enthusiasm and vision of the good life could do to resolve them.

Private companies in the fishing industry learned how to co-operate to ensure their survival. In 1945, National Sea Products brought together eighteen fishing companies. It soon learned to play the government grant game, putting larger and larger vessels, built with federal funds, into the waters of the Atlantic.

The success of the co-operative movement alarmed the private sector, which pressured the federal government to set up the Royal Commission on the Taxation of Cooperatives in 1944. A cartoon in the *Financial Post* of October 28 in that year showed how private business saw co-ops. The Dominion government, symbolized by a policeman, helps itself to a fruit stand representing the private sector. A nearby co-op store remains untouched. The caption asks, "Why does he always pick my store?" The attacks on co-ops, led by the insurance and retailing industries, identified them with socialism. Co-ops distributed their surpluses as rebates that were not taxed. Private business wanted this changed.

The year 1944 marked the hundredth anniversary of the English Rochdale co-op store, an event that spread awareness of the origin and history of the co-operative movement. It had started because of the way private business exploited consumers.

The Royal Commission forced the members of the Antigonish Movement and their allies to mobilize support and present their case to the government and all Canadians. As Laidlaw noted, "It was a jolt to the promoters of the co-operatives to learn that the movement was a closed book outside the circle of membership."

The brief that Coady presented to the Royal Commission gave him a much-needed chance to review the movement and set it into context. It was one of eleven presentations on the co-op movement in the Maritimes region. *The Social Significance of the Antigonish Movement* ran to 30 pages and was later reprinted as a pamphlet. Speaking with passion, he moved discussions about co-ops from nuts-and-bolts concerns to spiritual matters. For him, "something of much greater and deeper significance is being decided.... This is a stage in the struggle between the profit-motive system and the co-operative way of life." Co-ops were not just business ventures. They were operated for the social and economic betterment of people and to serve as a foundation of democracy by ensuring "the participation by the people in all vital and important social processes." Through individual and group ownership, co-ops were "a buffer between the individual and the omnipotent state. It is the last great democratic obstacle in the way of complete statism." Coady stressed the theme of universal brotherhood, one that he would mention many times in the future, and he linked co-ops and Christianity. These locally owned self-help ventures encouraged "charity and the practice of mercy, for the performance of which the Divine Master promised eternal life. [They are] the channels through which Christianity can operate in the world."

Coady at His Peak

> [Coady] had one shortcoming: he was strictly a rural person and therefore did not fully appreciate what was taking place, especially after World War II, in the massive move towards urbanization.
>
> —Alex Laidlaw, "The Coady-Tompkins Experience"

Coady held onto his vision of a better world through co-operation during the dark days of the war and its aftermath, as ruined nations strove to rebuild their economies and repair the tattered fabric of their social worlds. But the new forces that emerged during and after the conflict made sustaining hope more and more difficult. The world changed, but Coady's ideas and enthusiasm did not.

In 1948, the Maritimes had 431 credit unions with $8 million in assets, 200 co-op stores doing $10 million in annual business, a fisheries wholesaler (UMF) and 241 co-op houses built or under construction. This substantial achievement heartened Coady and his followers. But in terms of the economy of the region, these self-help ventures were drops in an ocean dominated by the private sector and government. The Allies had won the war through the hierarchical command and control system, which centralized power in a few hands and gave them access to huge quantities of resources. Bigger had proved to be better in running the affairs of democratic nations. Laidlaw believed that although Coady sympathized with urban workers, "I don't think his heart was with labour unions in the same way as with rural organizations of farmers and fishermen."

The rural population kept declining, despite the best efforts of Coady and his followers. In 1941, agriculture employed 26 per cent of the labour force in the Maritimes. Twenty years later, the figure was 5.6 per cent, and farm production had barely increased. Many rural dwellers made a living from a little bit of this and a little bit of that – fishing, subsistence farming, working in the woods or on the roads, driving school buses. In small communities where ancient feuds divided people, residents cherished their individualism and whatever control they had over their lives.

In urban areas, unions gave members a sense of community and collective power. To Coady, these organizations formed part of the old antagonistic economic system that pitted "workers" against "bosses." In his new society, everyone would be both. The priest's views on organic communities still found a ready reception among his university colleagues and the priests in the region, as Laidlaw noted:

> They were mainly rural in their outlook, and if you spoke of
> the inevitability of urbanization, then you had to be ready for
> a heated argument. This was a deficiency in the Antigonish
> program in the beginning: the leaders did not fully understand
> the urban point of view.

But he pointed out that Alex MacIntyre, Father Mike MacKinnon (who succeeded Coady in 1952) and Father Joe A. MacDonald, who came from the industrial area of Cape Breton, did much to counter the rural bias of the movement. Laidlaw believes that Coady was at the height of his power and influence in 1949. A photo shows him with Alex MacIntyre and Roy Bergengren in that year. Coady stands between the two men, who have just received honorary degrees from St. F.X. He stares straight at the camera, hands clasped, feet apart, looking as solid as an ancient oak.

Several developments had taken place at the university that appeared to advance Coady's cause. In 1941, St. F.X. introduced a two-year diploma in social and co-operative leadership, giving academic credibility to a process that had previously been done in an ad hoc and spontaneous manner. The program did not attract many people, and the first diploma was not awarded until 1947. In March 1943, radio station CJFX went on the air. This private venture had been supported by St. F.X. to expand the scope of the Extension Department. Through programs such as "The University of the Air" and "Labour School of the Air," CJFX provided information to study groups on health, home economics, and social and economic conditions.

In June 1946, the Vatican tapped Coady's talents. He went to Washington to buy $150,000 worth of wheat for Pope Pius XII to distribute to hungry people in Europe. Canadian Catholics raised this money, and the funds were deposited to Coady's credit – a striking example of the trust that everyone had in him. While in the American capital, he spoke with relief officials, pointing out how the methods of his movement could be applied in war-shattered lands. The Extension Department, he assured them, could respond to "a series of SOS calls...to investigate possibilities and change them into actualities."

In the post-war years, Coady recognized that his movement had become "big and complicated" but remained "promising." He wanted fishermen to become more "scientifically minded" even as unions strove to recruit them.

At that time, the Antigonish Movement did the 180-degree turn that characterizes such ventures. In the 1930s, its followers sought to disrupt the established order, to subvert capitalism by organizing people into collectivities. Now it strove to stabilize life in small communities, to oppose the evils of godless communism, which was gaining ground, by encouraging local self-help projects.

While staying true to his broad vision of the good society, Coady spent a lot of time developing the fisheries. The needs here were obvious. Fishermen had to provide good-quality products on a sustained basis to buyers. This meant better organization, more sophistication about markets, some degree of specialization, and the introduction of new technologies for processing and freezing fish. The fishermen still needed Coady's leadership, and he became their inspirer and problem solver as he had been in the barnstorming years.

The co-operative movement in Canso had experienced difficulties. The credit union had failed and the co-op store struggled to stay in business. Here, where the movement that Coady led had begun, the residents called on him to sort out their problems. In January 1948, he and Alex "Tando" MacIsaac of his department drove over icy roads to Whitehead. During the difficult journey, as Tando strove to keep the car on the road, Coady talked about what needed to be done in Canso. He also offered advice to the driver. As the car skidded or spun sideways, Coady would clutch his chest and cry, "Oh, God! My heart!"

Coady and Tando met with the fishermen in small groups. Ever optimistic, the priest saw them "getting down to brass tacks." Then they addressed a larger meeting. After an introduction by Father Forest from Larry's River, Coady slipped into his usual way of speaking, his fingers and arms moving as he began to jab his listeners with his "hypodermic needle." He did not worry about upsetting the fishermen: "They're good fellows with keen intellects and they can take it." To progress, he told the audience, they had to have scientific knowledge, co-operative action and strength of character if they were to retain their role as pioneers of a new economy and a more just society. This presentation at Whitehead was followed by a meeting with the co-operative fishery in Canso. Beset by problems and in financial difficulty, it needed Coady's enthusiasm and contacts to survive. The wharf and the storage and processing facilities were in poor condition and had to be replaced. This would cost $13,000. How much money could the co-op contribute? asked Coady. Only $4,000, came the reply. Coady told the co-op members that he could arrange a loan of $9,000 from the credit union in Antigonish.

Then Coady and Tando went off to address a mass meeting. It was just like the old days! Tando began with a stinging analogy:

> Among the animals, the dog is the one animal that can be kicked and booted by his master and when everything is over, still look up trustingly into the face of his master. The dog has nothing on those who will not follow the co-operative way but prefer to stick to the old slave-like system.

Despite a rousing ovation when he stood up to speak, Coady began awkwardly. He joked about the ride with Tando. Then his voice rose as he spoke about familiar themes and enthralled his audience:

> You have tasted the economic blood and it has turned you into a new breed of fighting men. Keep moving forward and nobody can stop you. You're now on the proper wavelength of progress, moving to a new and perpetual crescendo of life.

He paused, then gave them some advice:

You need to study, to get more scientific knowledge, more know-how, a better grasp of the co-operative philosophy, and to build yourselves into powerful men of learning and of character.

His poetic vision of the future of the fisheries was spiked with humour:

There is more wealth in this blue prairie sea in front of us than in the lush Niagara peninsula or the vast and fertile prairies of Western Canada, and not even a damned grasshopper.

Then came the final message:

We are all accustomed to the sea in these Maritime provinces. The roar of the sea is ever in our ears. We have fought with the invulnerable tides and I hope we are taking on the pugnacity of this adversary. Let this old sea with the coming and going of its tides teach us a lesson.

Coady used new words such as "wavelengths" in his talk, derived from his experiences with CJFX. In later years, he would refer to primary producers and workers as "the human atoms of society." Fused through economic co-operation, they would have the power of an H-bomb. Yet he could also quote from the Gospel of St. Luke and pass on Christ's advice to his apostles when they reported a poor fishing trip to him: "Put out into the deep and lower your nets for a catch." Coady had an extraordinary capacity to lift the spirits of his listeners.

After the meeting in Canso, he and Tando went on to the Dover to give another presentation. Then they loaded the car on a ship to take it to Mulgrave. From there, Tando drove back to Antigonish, arriving late at night.

The next day, Coady arrived at his office at his usual hour of nine, answered three letters, then went to the credit union to negotiate the $9,000 loan he had promised the Canso fishing co-op. Contacted by phone, the members of the credit committee approved the loan. Back in his office, he called the staff in for afternoon tea: "I think you people should get the benefit of a good breeze from the Canso coast." He told his people of "the happiest week of my whole existence." At the age of 66, the Coady charisma still worked.

On January 19, he wrote enthusiastically to C.C. Wilson, Supervisor of Instruction in the federal Department of Fisheries:

My wildest dreams about the Canso coast and about the whole Eastern Shore of Nova Scotia are coming true. We can solve this problem as you can see by this letter – as a matter of fact, they are being solved now – Port Bickerton to Larry's River being the answer. I never got such a thrill in my life.

The letter describes how the Canso people had begun to revitalize their fishing co-operative. But he notes that Father Jimmy "has not been working with us too harmoniously in the last few years. He is hipped on regional libraries as the sole manner of education for adults." Tompkins recognized the dangers of the movement becoming rigid, inflexible and formalized. While his campaign for regional libraries where anyone could find the best knowledge possible to solve their problems was not successful, it offered an alternative to Coady's approach.

The trip to Canso proved to be Coady's last hurrah as the fixer and friend of the fishermen. He continued to run his department, to speak, write and travel and promote his ideas. He knew the shape of the future and the perils that lay ahead for his movement. But he also knew that he had to keep up the spirits of his people while disturbing them with his prods to keep them thinking and acting. He wanted everyone to tackle their problems with the courage and vigour that marked his life.

Some small attempts had been made in eastern Nova Scotia to create health co-operatives and prepaid health insurance plans. Coady recognized that such initiatives could not take the place of government action. In September 1947, he addressed the annual meeting of the Nova Scotia Federation of Labour in Trenton. On the night before his address, he had a curious and unsettling experience:

Last night I was visited by an old Margaree neighbour, the man who met me at the Inverness station the time my mother died. He himself has been dead for many years, but there he was as plain as day standing at the foot of my bed at two o'clock this morning. He didn't say anything – he just stood there – and I know I was awake because as soon as he left I picked up my "nugget book" from the table beside my bed and wrote some notes in it. This morning I offered Mass for him. Poor fellow! I hope he's all right.

Father Topshee came to pick up Coady to drive him to Trenton. Coady welcomed him, telling him that he had forgotten to shave, and asking him to wait while he went off to do so. As Topshee drove westward, Coady rehearsed his speech. "They're a hard-boiled crowd and they need to be spurred into action, so I'm going to shock them out of their apathy toward my proposal for a co-operative health program,"he said. Nearing their destination, Topshee glanced at Coady and noticed that his face and hands had turned black. He had used silver nitrate – which he kept in his medicine cabinet, perhaps to darken his hair – instead of aftershave lotion. The two frantic men could find no remedy for Coady's blackness in New Glasgow. In nearby Trenton, the audience was surprised to see a big black man mount the platform. Coady explained "the stupid things I did this morning after I shaved this face of mine" before launching into his speech.

Then he laid the rawhide whip on his audience. He told the mining leaders who were present of his disappointment at the failure of his efforts in industrial Cape Breton to develop a co-operative health plan. Instead of working together, the miners had squabbled:

> You fellows had a chance to develop the best possible program,
> but you allowed yourselves to be divided and weakened by
> all sorts of propaganda and vicious prejudice. You had your
> chance and you blew it.

The labour leaders had to "pull together as one great force" and pressure the government to provide hospital and medical services.

This speech marked a shift in Coady's thinking. He realized that, on its own, his bottom-up approach to change would not create the kind of society he envisaged. It had to be complemented by efforts from the top down. In 1949, he spoke at co-operative rallies in Saskatchewan and was greeted with a "tornado of applause." The people of the province had elected a Co-operative Commonwealth Federation government in 1944, headed by Tommy Douglas, another charismatic clergyman. With his cabinet, Douglas began to work towards the creation of a socialist society, planning to usher in a new era of democratic government. In the early 1950s, Coady wrote, "I think Saskatchewan is leading the way in Canada.... With all due respect to my American friends, I really think that the U.S.A. will be the last country in the free world to get democracy."

After the meeting in Trenton, Coady was scheduled to give another talk on medicare. First he visited Father Clarke, a physics professor known for coping with crises. Clarke burst out laughing when he saw the black-faced priest. Coady shouted, "Stop laughing and tell me if you have anything that will clear up this mess!" Clarke dabbed sodium thiosulphate on Coady's face and the black man became white again.

7

The Lion in Winter

Social betterment [is] so easy to perceive, but difficult to reduce to statistics.

—Moses Coady

After 1949, Coady's life began to change. He still ran the Extension Department, his talents as a leader obvious to all, but he had few opportunities for hands-on work at the grassroots level. He had become something of an icon; a certain nostalgia arose about the old days of the 1930s when he and his colleagues struggled so hard with so few resources to liberate farmers, fishermen and workers from poverty and oppression.

Honours came to Coady now, and he travelled extensively to speak to groups who admired his work. The co-operative and credit union movement flourished, although the study-group approach to their development fell by the wayside in the mid-'50s. Coady always saw beyond the numbers in his movement. To him it was about changing the hearts and minds of men and women, developing their potential for good so that they could work together for the betterment of themselves and their communities. He proposed a people's research institute to study some of the immediate and long-term problems that beset eastern Nova Scotia, as more and more young people left for opportunities in other parts of Canada. It would come up with formulae and blueprints

– favourite words of Coady's – to keep these people in the region. Coady was always suspicious of theories and concepts unrelated to local realities: "There is a great danger in mere abstract thinking." Research would have helped him to allocate his scarce resources more effectively, but his proposal was not accepted.

In 1948, the Co-operative Education Extension Service of Philadelphia named Coady the Most Distinguished Co-operator, "the grand old man of Nova Scotia Co-operatives." The following year, he addressed the plenary session of the Economic and Social Council of the United Nations on "Organizing Rural People for the Proper Use and Conservation of Natural Resources."

Growing up in the Margaree, he had seen how the environment influenced life there, and how good husbandry made the land fruitful. In his speech to the UN, he claimed that environmental degradation arose from an ignorance of science, a lack of ownership of land by the masses and the greed of those motivated only by profit. These themes, familiar in our time, were new when Coady spoke. He became an ardent conservationist in his later years, claiming that we are "poisoning our earth and our waters.... We cannot sin against nature and hope to win.... Work with nature and nature will work with us." Always concerned with his health, he urged on others the virtues of using compost for growing better food. And he joyfully told his friends about his weight loss. As he aged, Coady went back to his roots, living on a simple, healthy diet and advocating the close relationship with nature that people in the Margaree had when he was a youth. Conservation also formed part of his concept of an organic society where all parts were interrelated and people lived in harmony with each other and with the land. Paradoxically, the efficiency and scientific approach that Coady so assiduously promoted meant that fewer and fewer hands were required on the farms, in the fisheries and in the woods.

One of Coady's dreams, land settlement, came about in the postwar years, but not in the way he envisaged it. With the help of Catholic clergy, Dutch immigrants were settling in eastern Nova Scotia. They had large families, a strong work ethic, love of the land, and the skills for turning poor land into good farms. They became successful farmers as more and more local residents went down the road to the expanding cities of Canada.

In 1949, the Canadian Association for Adult Education (CAAE) elected Coady its president. The organization used the listening-group process pioneered by Coady and his colleagues in their radio forums.

Citizens learned about social and economic matters as once the members of the study groups had. On September 1, 1949, Ned Corbett and Coady addressed the Royal Commission on National Development in the Arts, Letters and Sciences (the Massey Commission) on the value of adult education and the co-operative movement. The commission's report mentioned "a precise and detailed statement" by the Canadian Association for Adult Education on how commercially sponsored radio affected its "field of interest."

About half of the peak listening period on the CBC was devoted to commercial radio supported by advertising:

> When an important national advertiser wanted the programme time of the *Citizen's Forum*, the C.B.C., we were told, moved that programme: against the expressed views of its listeners to an hour inconvenient for most families.

Sponsors objected to any talk or program of a serious nature for at least an hour before their program began. Coady, Corbett and other leaders in popular adult education, meanwhile, had quickly grasped the potential of radio. Through radio, everyone could have access to the best minds in Canada and the world now that sets were cheap and readily available.

In co-operation with the CBC, the CAAE developed outstanding community radio programs. The National Farm Radio Forum had been well received by rural people. It served as a model for other countries that used its approach in their local development programs to inform and involve people in the decision-making process. The activists in CAAE slowly lost ground to those members who saw adult education as being directed at personal development and individual advancement. Coady and others of like mind had to contend not only with the desire of private business to use radio as a way of promoting their products and services, but also with governments that had a skeptical view of their work in adult education.

Coady was a leading proponent of the approach to community development that linked co-operative development with adult education. In 1940, the CBC and the CAAE planned a fifteen-minute talk by Coady in a radio series entitled "Inquiry into Cooperation." Business people and boards of trade in the west saw the broadcasts as "inimical to private enterprise." They demanded that the series be cancelled before Coady spoke. Prime Minister Mackenzie King, facing an election, pressured the CBC to do so, and Coady was informed that his talk, scheduled for

February 1940, was cancelled. The move backfired. Judith Robinson, a *Globe and Mail* columnist, blasted the Prime Minister: "Co-operation is, it seems, too dangerous an ideal to be given the freedom of the air while Mr. King is holding an election." After praising Coady and his movement, Robinson added, "Co-operation is not the sort of ideal that the CBC can afford to cherish on Government-controlled airwaves at election time."

The CBC reversed its decision, and Coady spoke to 400 study groups in the west, 2,390 in the Maritimes, as well as other interested listeners. The rest of the series on co-operatives was postponed until April.

During and after the war, the ability of big business to influence politics, the increasing power and reach of the central government, and the rise of liberal individualism became increasingly marked and touched even the remotest parts of Nova Scotia. After the war, as the economy boomed, jobs were plentiful and consumerism accelerated. Coady saw the power of the consumer as a crucial factor in changing society. But consumers refused to exercise the power of the shopping basket. Federal and provincial governments created the welfare state, putting safety nets under poor and marginalized people and launching huge development schemes to generate jobs in Atlantic Canada and other "underdeveloped" regions of the country.

Alex Sim points out one of the post-war influences that changed how people lived and learned to interact. Canada's British tradition of pragmatism and collective action was slowly replaced by American idealism and individualism:

> The Antigonish Movement had a strong cerebral thrust. It combined heads, hearts and hands to encourage people to take charge of their own destinies. In the late Forties, group dynamics became popular. People talked about how they felt about each other. Encounter groups, Esalen, sensitivity training and other techniques emphasized the spiritual side of human development. They attempted to resolve the tensions between people's heads and their hearts, between their intellects and their emotions. Education programs that encouraged people to ask questions created alarm.

The approach of the study clubs – "Listen. Study. Discuss. Act." – was blunted by this new form of group dynamics, which spread rapidly in the 1960s. People spent time listening, studying and discussing personal concerns without moving into action. Abraham Maslow's ideas about self-actualization also undercut efforts in community development. In some ways, Maslow's ideas resembled those of Coady, who wanted "bread before Brahms," but always saw his efforts as creating time for people to engage in cultural activities once their basic physical needs were met. But Coady knew that personal development could not take place in isolation: it had to be linked to efforts to enhance the well-being of others through co-operative ventures.

The efforts to generate development from the top down, through various forms of social engineering and government intervention into the lives of poor people, and from the bottom up, through group discussion, slowly sapped the energies, idealism and impulses that gave rise to the Antigonish Movement and sustained it through the difficult early days.

How much Coady recognized these new forces in development is not known. But nothing dampened his enthusiasm for co-operation and adult education and his belief in the potential of ordinary people. Yet he had a blind spot about culture, as his relations with the Acadians showed.

Coady and the Acadians

> [Coady] was a powerful orator and a writer of talent. But he was also fiercely Scottish, and I know from having lived it, that he spent a good part of his time eliminating Acadians from all important functions in his movement.

—Alexandre J. Boudreau, *À l'assaut des défis* (author's translation)

Boudreau came from Chéticamp, an Acadian community on the west coast of Cape Breton that had a long and strong tradition of self-help and co-operation. His reference to Coady's relationship with the Acadians reflects the fact that Coady twice tried to have Boudreau fired after he became an ag. rep. in 1934. Coady surrounded himself with like-minded people, playing a role somewhat like that of a clan chief. Boudreau operated in the same way, and like Coady took a broad view of his brief:

> I was instrumental in organizing the Chéticamp Credit Union, the Grand Etang Credit Union, the co-operative store… the fishermen in Chéticamp – while I was an agricultural rep. because you couldn't separate fishermen and farmers.

Deported in 1755 by the British for remaining neutral in the struggle between them and the French, the Acadians who stayed in the region, or trickled back into it, developed a unique culture. Highly skilled in agriculture, they blended individual effort with collective endeavours that strengthened and sustained their small communities. The Chéticantins organized a fish marketing co-op, the first in the region, in 1915. Boudreau worked to encourage co-ops in the same way that Coady did. From 1923 on, Lillian Burke, a New Yorker, spent the summers in Cape Breton. She visited Chéticamp, and helped hooked-rug makers there to improve their products. She sold the rugs in the United States; the makers received very little for them. The outsider, while helpful in making the rugs more marketable, occupied the traditional role of the merchant, making money from the fingers of the workers. While recognizing that she was rendering a great service to the people of Chéticamp, and bringing much-needed cash into the community, the rug-makers became upset about the low returns they were receiving. Boudreau met with them and supported them in confronting Burke. They demanded to be paid a dollar per square foot for their work. Burke refused, so Boudreau suggested that they organize to sell their rugs themselves. A number of the rug-hookers formed an informal group and found an agent to market their work, while others stayed faithful to Burke, who went to court to claim ownership of the rug designs. Boudreau hired a lawyer from Inverness who defeated this move. Boudreau acted very much as Coady would have done, organizing exploited people to gain more control over their lives, and the Chéticantin stated in an interview that he saw his work as forming part of the Antigonish Movement.

Coady had warm personal relationships with many Acadian priests, but he did not seem to grasp the importance of French to the Acadians. Boudreau claims that Coady "was not an easy man to deal with" and confronted him when he appointed a fieldworker who spoke only English to direct the study clubs that he had set up in Mabou. Boudreau, who had all the priests and the local people behind him in this matter, said he was going to tell Coady's appointee to stay home. And he prevailed in his opposition to the appointment. In 1936 Coady appointed the department's first French-speaking fieldworker, but the movement never produced any material in French, and Boudreau had to translate what came from Antigonish for the study groups. Coady was not anti-Acadian. His attitude towards these people reflected that of Bishop Morrison, who lamented, "It's hard enough to teach religion in one language without trying to teach it in two."

In 1938, Boudreau became professor of adult education and co-operative organizations at the School for Agriculture and Fisheries at Sainte-Anne-de-la-Pocatière in Quebec. Here he organized the United Fishermen of Quebec, a federation of 38 co-operatives with 4,000 members. Continually frustrated at the lack of learning material in French, the people of Chéticamp, with the help of a Quebec organization, held a mass meeting in 1947. The co-op store and the fishermen's co-op became separate entities. Increasingly, the Acadians drew upon material from Quebec, especially on the *caisses populaires*, the people's banks launched by Alphonse Desjardins in 1900.

Boudreau identified himself as a "nationalist," a word that irked Coady. "I have no axe to grind about the Antigonish Movement," stated Boudreau. "It was the biggest thing that ever happened in eastern Nova Scotia." But Coady failed to draw upon the knowledge and experience of collective action that the Acadians had acquired through two centuries of oppression. Like all charismatic leaders, Coady saw his movement as leading to an ideal society, run rationally and efficiently. Anything, or anyone, that did not fit into this blueprint was seen as a threat.

The tensions between Coady and the Acadian leaders were exacerbated by money matters. After the war ended, Acadians in Chéticamp and New Brunswick joined with fishermen from Quebec to organize community education programs in French. They asked the Extension Department for some of the funds it received from Ottawa for this. The request infuriated Coady.

He went to Ottawa to demand that his department be recognized as the centre for co-op training and development in the Maritimes. The Department of Fisheries backed the Extension Department's monopoly. On his return to Antigonish, Coady wrote to one of his challengers, denouncing "the sudden injection of nationalistic spirit into the situation." Nothing he had "ever written, or said, or done...would convict me of an anti-French bias.... The promotion of separate cultures is likely to involve measures of friction and diversity."

Yet a certain vindictiveness characterized Coady's attitudes towards Acadian leaders. In his 1948 letter to C.C. Wilson, he mentioned going to Moncton "to do a little scouting around," as the French had held a meeting "on this National question." He hoped "the thing may be settled amicably."

Before travelling to Moncton, Coady wrote to Father Michael Gillis, in whom he often confided. The Acadians who would be at the meeting were "all skunks, but the world can't seem to get along without a little smell," he said. He called the Acadian leaders "well-heeled manipulators." In Moncton, Coady defended the record of his department, while admitting that more could have been done to provide material and services in French. Later, he identified to his friend Father J.L. Chiasson "the Canadian problem" – the creation of trust and understanding between English and French. Coady appeared unaware that his attitude was eroding this process. Somehow, he failed to recognize that community development required a sense of identity based on shared values and on local pride in local culture. To him, culture was all about opera and classical music, not about the unique way in which people lived, worked and thought.

Increasingly, the Acadians went their own way.

In March 1954, Coady wrote to Father Mike MacKinnon, his successor, complaining that, over the past five years, none of the top members in Extension had been invited to address meetings in French-speaking areas, even though "in the first years they took our doctrines with great rejoicing." Using co-ops and education for narrow purposes "defeated the whole program." In the same month, Coady wrote to Dr. Stewart Bates, Deputy Minister of Fisheries, who had hired several Acadian fieldworkers. He praised these men. Although they were not "Anglo Saxon," they had been "Caledonized – In their wisdom and strategy they are close seconds to our own smart Scottish race." Coady may have been joking, but his comment lends point to Boudreau's statement about Coady being "fiercely Scottish" – despite his Irish origins.

Retirement

> The rank and file of the world's people are not going to be fooled any longer, and when the right time comes they will put up new guillotines to cut off the stupid heads of the leaders in Church and State who are incapable of seeing where the real danger is and who are lacking in courage to apply an adequate remedy.
>
> —Moses Coady to Father Michael Gillis (1954)

Two themes emerge in Coady's life and thought in his last decade. On the surface he remained the optimistic, open and cheerful individual he had always been. But disappointment and some bitterness began to appear as he looked at the world around him. His vision had conjured up a blueprint for the ideal society: but why were people not paying attention to it? For a man like Coady, constantly dreaming beyond the mountain, always convinced that ordinary people could do so much more to change their destinies, the follies and human weaknesses that he encountered locally and on his journeys made him sad. Human beings persisted in being human, rather than striving to be godlike.

In the meantime, his health became more and more precarious. In 1952 he had a major heart attack and was cursed with gallstones. On February 5 of that year, he wrote to his bishop, resigning his position as director of the Extension Department, saying, "Age and infirmities forced me to this decision." He was now 70 years old, and had driven himself hard all his life.

Apparently, he did not think his resignation would be accepted, but it was. As the news spread, Coady was deluged with tributes. He wrote to his sister-in-law that "a fellow never knows how popular he is until he is about to die – but I have been used to this so long that my hat fits the same as usual." From St. Martha's Hospital, where he was recovering from an attack of gallstones, he wrote to his niece Teresa: "My resignation…has called forth a lot of eulogies which, of course, a man of my modesty and stability does not notice at all." Through dieting, he lost over 20 pounds: "I am getting good looking again but I am feeling really wonderfully well," he noted. The only thing wrong was "that the rhythm of my heart is destroyed." He'd had this condition before "but got back on the rails." Coady's good humour and exuberance shines through these letters.

He knew his work and ideas would endure. Leaders in adult education and co-operatives in the United States signed testimonials that were bound into a book. In 1953, he received a tribute and a gift from the Nova Scotia Division of Adult Education. He responded: "I haven't accumulated much else but friends and they are from all over the world…. I guess in that sense I am the richest man in the world."

In retirement, Coady wrote, delivered addresses, served as god-father at the Extension Department and welcomed visitors. He noted, "I…get a great thrill in meeting these men. One of the most enjoyable features of my life in the last few years has been my work with scores of people who come from all over the world to study our Extension program." Photos of Coady with visitors show a happy, contented man. He was back doing what he loved – teaching people, sharing his knowledge, assuring them of their potential for making a better world through co-operation.

In June 1952, Emory Bogardus, a professor from the University of Southern California, met with Coady and wrote a paper on him and the movement. He described the origins of the movement in the 1930s:

> Fishermen, coal miners and steel workers, and farmers were developing attitudes of desperation. They had energy, undeveloped mental capacities, the desires and longings of normal human beings for a better life, and yet they were failing to obtain the necessities of life.

Agitators invaded communities, "declaring that violence was the needed solution." After paying tribute to Father Jimmy Tompkins, the writer describes the achievements of the co-operative movement:

> They are learning how to organize...associations on the basis of private property and the freest form of enterprise known to man, with a minimum aid from government. Since mutual self-help and responsibility are the keynote, statism is opposed by co-operatives.

Coady enthusiastically promoted his blueprint of the good society to the visitor. He identified four classes of co-op activity: retail and wholesale co-ops; credit unions; co-operative processing, marketing and production; and "services, including housing, hospital services, library services."

Bogardus, as so many other commentators on the movement had done, identified the small discussion groups as the key to its success. But at the time of his visit, these were losing their lustre and appeal. In the 1930s, people had come together to talk about what interested them. Now study groups dealt with specific topics, offering less of a social occasion. Radio programs delivered information to the study group, backed up with printed matter. The Extension Department had a collection of coloured slides of co-operative activities that circulated in the region. Young people were encouraged to learn about co-ops through essay writing, public speaking and debating contests in schools. But now Nova Scotians had other diversions. Radio, television, shopping malls and booming cities drew people whose nights out in the past had revolved around a study club session.

Coady told his visitor that he still hoped that the experiment he had begun in the Margaree would improve human well-being, and that his methods could be "universalized as far as they are applicable."

His health improved during the mid-'50s. He believed this was due to salmon and strawberries from the Margaree. But when he returned there, Coady saw how empty the land had become. The Margaree credit union failed. More and more young people left Nova Scotia for the good life that Coady envisaged they could have created at home through self-help and mutual aid. He saw his nephew Leo revitalizing his beloved Margaree and as "part of my dream of building a new society within this part of the world." But the young man had his own ideas about his future, and followed the usual path of feckless rural youth. He drove cars at high speed on rural roads, crashing them from time to time, and developed a drinking problem. Coady constantly admonished him to mend his ways, remain sober and manage his affairs efficiently. Sadly, Coady concluded that Leo "just hasn't got what it takes." Although his nephew did eventually straighten out his life and settle down, he could never be the leader that his uncle craved. Leo could only be the man he was, not a construction of the gifted person who had risen from humble origins in the Margaree to international prominence.

Just before he retired, Coady visited Europe. He wrote to a friend, "Things are very bad over there. France and England were never so near financial collapse – poverty everywhere and imminent danger of war and revolution."

But he hoped a better world would come out of this turmoil. The key word was "brotherhood," and Coady became a powerful proponent of the concept. He had shown how the word could be made flesh through his movement.

The vitality of the man and his vision impressed Bogardus, who drew upon Coady's ideas to end his paper:

> The Antigonish Movement, being still young and dynamic, has vast possibilities before it. It indicates that co-operation is more than business; it is "the ultimate in justice." It is a force for brotherhood and it gives unity of thought and action to any mosaic of peoples. It transforms a community into a family. It creates good will and fair dealings – essentials for world peace.

After retiring as Extension director, Coady became its "idea man." In 1953, the department had a staff of 25, and strong support from Bishop John R. MacDonald, who took office in 1950. But the department was $155,000 in the red. St. F.X. began playing up its role in defeating communism as a way of raising its profile – and, presumably, its funding. An article in *Maclean's* on June 1, 1953, claimed that "SFX has put new life into a dying fishing industry, restored idle farms and stamped out Communism in industrial Cape Breton, once a hot-bed of radical activity."

The bishop replaced Coady with "Father Mike" – Michael J. MacKinnon – a quiet, shy son of a coal miner from Cape Breton. Coady had made him director of labour classes on the island in 1948, and head of the Extension office in Sydney two years later. He credited Father Mike with routing communists from the region.

Although MacKinnon had the experience he needed for the job, Coady proved to be a hard act to follow. As the university's historian put it: "It is surely rare to find so many leadership qualities – energy, oratory, imagination, vision, commitment, service, optimism, and courage – combined in one person." Father Mike, like his mentor, was a fighter for justice and the little people. But he lacked Coady's skills in mediation and his warm humanity. A Carnegie official described the new director as "an intelligent and forceful person but without Coady's imagination and social grace." Unlike his predecessor, MacKinnon failed to relate well to his staff and key people outside the department. An extension worker claimed that MacKinnon exhibited a "bulldozing fighting spirit" when dealing with the Department of Agriculture and "a disregard for the point of view of other institutions."

In 1956, a venture for which Coady had pressed came into being with the creation of Eastern Cooperative Services. An integrated wholesale venture for the region, ECS also became a strong player in the agriculture sector. It was, in Coady's words, "the synthesis of all the things we have been working at in the past twenty eight years." And the Extension Department acquired a research capability with the appointment of Desmond Connor, a New Zealander, to its staff in 1957. Among other things, he began to study rural migration. He worked in the same spirit that Coady had pioneered: "I was given a very free hand. I started a little noon radio program once a week on CJFX…to foster new approaches."

Working with ECS, Connor encouraged blueberry-growing. He notes: "Dr. Coady was still around and active then. He often came into my office, sat down and just watched me working. He kept saying, to my embarrassment, that I would go far."

Coady still believed in the potential of every person he met. Connor indeed became a leading authority and enabler in community development and public participation in Canada and all over the world. Connor found Father Mike "a bit of a wild man – lots of energy, always on the move, difficult to get him to sit down and plan or prepare a speech for an important occasion."

Alex Laidlaw, until he went to India to work with the Reserve Bank in 1956, focused on policy issues, striving to sort out the messages of the movement that were relevant to a new era. Archie Maclean visited fishing communities, and Ellen Arsenault "as executive secretary, really kept the operation on track. Sr. Marie Michael was a delightful soul, but stuck to her library." The teamwork approach that had made Coady's efforts so rewarding seems to have vanished under his successor. A steady stream of international visitors had to be greeted, briefed and taken on field trips, but "this became very time-consuming and made effective field visits very difficult."

Connor, however, believes that the Antigonish Movement was still working well when he left Extension in 1960. Two years before this, Bishop MacDonald pressured the president of St. F.X. to remove Father Mike as its director. By this time, Laidlaw had followed in A.B. MacDonald's footsteps and gone to Ottawa to become general secretary of the Co-operative Union of Canada. Rev. John A. Gillis became director of Extension in 1958. He had been Father Jimmy Tompkins's curate in Reserve Mines, ran the college farm at Mount Cameron, and involved in co-operatives among farmers, fishermen and labourers.

Coady predicted that Gillis would be a "great success." But the new director had no experience of extension work and claimed that Coady "waxed hot and cold" in his attitude to him. Connor found Gillis "pretty traditional and not about to support anything new or different."

In a talk he gave on CBC-TV on July 8, 1957, Coady stated that he still stayed in his old quarters at the university, and "I have an office and take part in some phases of the extension work. I make the odd speech and lecture at short courses." He was spending a lot of time with visitors from Africa, South America, the Caribbean and Asia.

> It is interesting to notice how some of the things we take for granted are new to them. I can say in all modesty that invariably they find here what they think may be the solution of their problems back home. We are conquering feudalism through the Antigonish program, and feudalism still holds in serfdom the great masses of their people. They see here, too, a poor people rising from their poverty to a new level of economic and social life.

After his appointment, Gillis sought the views of people in the department on the extension program and how it could contribute to adult education and the co-op movement in the region. In his response, Coady railed against private-profit business, and warned Gillis of those enemies who were trying to water down the philosophy of extension that he had developed. If anyone interfered with the program to help people to control their own economic affairs, "it matters not who he is or what his position, we will fight him to the death." Even in the last years of his life, Coady retained his original vision and his passion for the little people he had so ably served. He did not, in the words of Dylan Thomas, go gentle into that good night.

At the End

> We go along the road of life – we turn a corner and suddenly there it is, the end of one's life. I wish that I had done things differently – better – and I wish I had done more.
>
> —Moses Coady

In his last years, Coady developed cataracts and wore a patch over one eye. He needed a cane to help him get around, and the staff of Extension remember its tapping sound as he walked along the office corridors.

The old guard of the movement faded away. A.B. MacDonald died in 1952, as did Alex MacIntyre. Father Jimmy became senile. After visiting his cousin and mentor in St. Martha's Hospital, Coady returned distressed. "I never want to see him again like that," he said. "I don't want to remember him like that." The fine mind and vigorous personality that had launched the Antigonish Movement had vanished, leaving a mere shell. Father Jimmy died in 1953.

Since childhood, Coady had seen the seasons change, and experienced life and death in a tightly knit rural community. Believing in the concept of an organic community where healthy new life replaced old growth, he accepted his ultimate demise with grace and courage. As the 1950s advanced, Coady suffered much pain from various afflictions, but kept his sense of humour. In 1956, he became anemic and learned that his blood was "only 60% normal." After receiving four transfusions of "Scotch blood," he informed a friend, "You may be sure that I will be growing more and more circumspect about my financial dealings in the future with all this Scotch blood in me."

His heart continued to trouble him. On May 8, 1958, he went to Madison, Wisconsin, to address the Credit Union National Association (CUNA). In the middle of the speech, his heart "gave way" and he collapsed and had to be carried out on a stretcher. As he put it to a friend: "Fortunately, my speech had been mimeographed and they passed around a thousand copies of it. I got across some good sections of it but I am afraid I was halting and labouring in doing it." After a spell in hospital, Coady returned to his hotel and then went to a conference of CUNA staff.

In 1959, he contracted pneumonia and received more blood transfusions. Laidlaw visited him in hospital:

> The huge machine was grinding slowly to its final halt. But his mind was as clear as ever – he dictated letters and notes almost to the end. He spoke a great deal of disappointments, of things that had not turned out as he had expected, of leaders who had failed in their trust, of those who had "let me down."

As his friend noted, "A social reformer and a dreamer of things as they might be can hardly remain cheerful to the last." Coady had become a skilled teacher who carried a message of hope to thousands of people: he helped them to change their lives and develop their potential and that of others. In his later years, he took on the role of the prophet, demanding that the powerful people in society serve God and the little people of the world. He took comfort in learning that his beloved nephew Leo had taken a job with a co-operative. On June 13, Coady wrote to Ida Delaney that his doctor had told him that he had only a little time to live and "I will be taking off pretty soon."

On Tuesday, July 28, 1959, Moses Coady phoned a few friends, had a light supper and then died peacefully. He was 77 years old. This deeply spiritual man strove to do God's work on earth. Like Saint Paul, facing death, he could say: "I have fought the good fight, I have finished my course, I have kept my faith." Nobody who knew this great Canadian could dispute that claim. Moses Michael Coady left behind the memory of a good man and a legacy of ideas and actions that are as relevant to our own times as they were to his.

8

The Living Legacy

There is an evergreen memory on the St. F.X. Campus of the old man with the eye patch and the walking cane who couldn't remember the names and dates of the honours heaped upon him but who proudly recited his high school Latin. There was a childish delight because some fisherman had named an insignificant boat after him while an appointment to high office would be forgotten in the inside pocket of his coat.
—Joseph Hernon, *The Atlantic Advocate*, February 1960

Alex Laidlaw recalled hearing of Coady's death while at a meeting in Saskatoon.

As one of our group…later described it, we felt that some kind of world had come to an end. And indeed it had – that world built on the Great Depression – the organization of study clubs, the emergence of adult education and the growing belief in those [Coady] called the "little people" and their power in organized groups.

Coady and his colleagues had operated in an elemental world of people living close to the land and sea, gaining a meagre existence from hard toil. The Second World War and the years after it brought greater security to the region as new technologies changed work in the fields, forests and fisheries. The rural world became much more complex as market forces grew stronger, enterprises (including co-operatives and credit unions) became larger, and the government got more and more involved in rescuing poor and marginalized peoples from the forces that stunted their lives.

Coady's approach to social change, his philosophy and his style of operation remain as vital and valuable today as they were in his time. People everywhere feel a sense of powerlessness as big business and big government dominate their lives. They struggle through the day to earn a living and make better lives for their children, frustrated by bureaucratic excesses in the state and private sectors. The gap between the governors and the governed – the democratic deficit – widens, as does that between rich and poor, the centres of power and its edges.

Coady, a visionary, recognized that development did not begin with building factories or luring industries to communities. It began in the hearts and minds of ordinary people. His ideas on economic democracy, co-operation, decentralization, respect for the environment, self-help, mutual aid, sound eating habits and other matters resonate through our own time.

To the end of his days, Coady presented a paradox. His great schemes for transforming the world had not come to fruition. He became impatient with those who failed to share his vision of a new society being born of human effort. Yet he continued to see potential in everyone he met. Malcolm MacLellan, a friend and fellow priest, noted the roots of Coady's being in a spirituality that "rose vertically to the infinite and extended horizontally to the world like a cross to embrace all people." The intersecting point on a cross marks the place of maximum tension, where the forces pulling people apart and those linking them together meet. Coady struggled to change society and the individuals comprising it. And sometimes he overstretched himself in this quest.

In his retirement, Coady focused his mind on communion with God: "I say Mass every day now. I have every spiritual happiness I can imagine, and I am glad to be able to carry on the kind of spiritual life that prepares me for a happy ending."

In his last days, wracked by illness, Coady told his bishop that he could now say *Nunc dimittis servum tuum, Domine*. These words – "Now, Lord, you can let your servant go in peace," spoken by the old man Simeon when the infant Jesus was presented at the temple in Jerusalem – reflected the priest's belief that his work was complete and that he could depart this life. "If I die," he said, "I die happy in the thought that my blueprint is being realized much more surely than I ever had a right to expect."

Coady's obituary in *The Casket* stated, "He spent his life doing good and the good that he did will live after him." Monsignor Frank MacKinnon, Coady's successor at Extension who died three months after his mentor, caught the paradox of this great Canadian:

> Always to me, he was one of the tall men, sun crowned, who live above the fog in public duty, and in private thinking. Above all else, he was Dr. M.M. Coady whose deep supernatural faith, basic simplicity and universal charity marked him as a most worthy priest.

The Halifax *Chronicle-Herald* noted how Coady's early environment nurtured his vision of the good life: "[He] never lost his child-like faith that, beneath it all, the world was as pure as the meadows of Nova Scotia's beautiful Margaree." The role that Coady played, still little recognized in our time, was that of a community entrepreneur, an enabler, facilitator and animator who pointed people towards a better life and helped them to reach it through their own efforts. An idealistic realist and realistic idealist, the priest knew how to motivate and energize people to get off their backsides and start doing something to improve their lives and other people's.

He had a simple faith in God and people – and a complex mind. He saw what he was doing as part of his priestly role, and that gave him his peculiar power – the ability to reach and understand people at their point of need and encourage them to start thinking and acting to bring into being a better world.

Coady's Grave

> Right Rev. M.M.Coady.
> Jan 3, 1882–July 28, 1959
>
> —Inscription on Coady's grave

On a muggy day in July 2002, I went in search of Coady's grave in St. Ninian's cemetery in Antigonish. His remains lie across the Trans-Canada Highway from the international learning institute at St. Francis Xavier University that bears his name.

I had great difficulty finding the grave. After spending an hour wandering among the ornate tombs of bishops, the small white gravestones of the Marthas and the plain monuments to MacDonalds, Chisholms, MacPhersons and Frasers, the little people whom Coady and his colleagues served so well, I finally asked a worker for directions. "Coady's grave is over there, with a bunch of priests' stones," he told me.

Two fishermen, two farmers, a steelworker and a miner carried Coady's coffin to this humble grave, marked only by a black marble slab carrying his name and the dates of his birth and death. From this place, you see a panorama of the land he loved, forested hills and small farms sweeping to the horizon, the sea sparkling in the distance.

* * *

Even at its height, the Antigonish Movement involved only a few thousand Nova Scotians. The need for tough-minded men like Coady and Tompkins emerges in Alden Nowlan's stories of growing up in rural Nova Scotia. Born in 1933, the poet developed a love of books – a practice seen by others as a waste of good drinking time. Dropping out of school in Grade 5 to work in the woods with his father, who earned a dollar a day, Nowlan entered a macho world. Boozing, wenching and brawling occupied weekends and spare time, even after the war. Women were supposed to know their place and keep to it. As Nowlan put it,

> It was a strong race. Generations of poverty and hard work had convinced them that the weak were invariably the first to perish. So they were pathetically afraid of tenderness.... One of the things I hated most when I was a child was how resigned my people were ... they were resigned because they were uninvolved. In the rural slum where I was born and grew up, nobody felt involved in the way society functioned. The government was just something that happened to you, like sickness or the weather.

During the Second World War, Canon Russell Elliott, a newly ordained minister, helped to form the Anglican Fellowship for Social Action. "The Briefcase Boys," as they were known from their habit of toting them around, "knew all about the Antigonish Movement and Moses Coady. Each of us in our parishes, in our own individual way, became supportive, using the Movement's services to further our own programs." The group came under attack for "being unfaithful to our Church since promoting the Antigonish Movement was actually promoting the Roman Catholic Church. [We were called] communists, traitors, pro-Roman because we understood our own personal loyalty, faith and vocation."

The area in which Elliott served, Cumberland County, fell into decline. In the summer of 1945, the descendants of Protestants and new

Danish settlers invited Coady to help them. He had an almost mythi-
cal status at that time. The awestruck Elliott drove him to a meeting at
Wallace Station:

> It was a first-hand opportunity to experience the impact of
> this very ordinary looking, heavy-set personality. An outsider
> might have had difficulty in distinguishing him at all, as he
> sat among farmers and fishermen. His language was no aca-
> demic cultured book-language but as salty and homespun as
> any in the room. It was full of briefly clipped statements and
> questions, and loaded with exclamation marks. He had never
> surrendered his Cape Breton farm-boy attitude or accent.

The meeting agreed to form a co-op store. A man with a strong
Danish accent spoke up: "We don't know how to do these things. You
come and start the store for us." Coady shot back: "By damn, you start it
yourselves!" Then he told them what they had to do – elect an interim
board of directors and start signing up members. As Elliott put it, "The
meeting ended with more hope than despair" and the co-op store opened
the following year.

The Anglican minister drove Coady back to Pugwash in pitch-
black darkness. The lights in the rickety vehicle went out as it descended
a hill overlooking the Northumberland Strait. Fiddling with the fuse,
Elliott made the lights work. They shone on the waters of the strait,
towards which the car was headed.

> I turned apologetically to Dr. Coady. He had his hat in his
> hand, fanning his face, and he exclaimed, in the strongest
> Cape Breton-Scottish accent I had heard him use all week: "My
> Gawd, and me with a heart condition!" He was real after all!

Elliott knew what constituted the priest's heart condition: "[It] had
always belonged to us ordinary, everyday Nova Scotians."

Deconstructing Coady and the Movement

> The best is the enemy of the good.
>
> —Ancient Greek axiom

When you talk with those who knew and worked with Coady,
their eyes light up, their faces glow and the words pour forth about the
joyful times they had with him. In recent years, the man and the movement he led have come under critical scrutiny by academics.

In reviewing Michael Welton's scholarly biography of Moses Coady in *Catholic New Times* (May 20, 2001), Jim Cameron, the historian of St. F.X. and the Marthas, praises it as a "solid, admirable 280-page historical study [that] brings Coady to life." In the last chapter of *Little Moisie from Margaree*, Welton calls the priest to task, as Cameron notes: "Thus Coady was racist, probably anti-Semitic, anthropocentric, ethnocentric, manipulative, dogmatic, self-deluded, a fastidious fusspot, a busybody, naive, a modernist rationalist and apolitical" and a "formidably flawed prophet." Interestingly, Welton seems to have derived his information on Coady mainly from documents and written records, rather than speaking to anyone who knew the man.

Debra Murphy called her master's thesis, submitted to Dalhousie University in 1975, *The Failure of the Antigonish Movement in Larry's River, Nova Scotia*. She set Coady's work into the theoretical framework of utopianism and ideas on the creation of new societies. Her thesis is based on what happened when Father Charles Forest moved to the small fishing village on the eastern shore in the 1930s and became the champion of co-operation. Residents established a cannery in 1933, a credit union in 1934 and a co-op store in 1936. Wartime brought labour shortages and higher prices for fish. In 1958, a report to the board of the cannery noted that some fishermen were leaving the industry and others were supporting competitors. Federal government regulations changed the size of lobsters that could be canned. The cannery ran out of them as private companies expanded their operations in the fisheries. Environmental changes along the Guysborough coast resulted in a decline in fish catches. Trawlers caught more fish in the offshore as the market moved from canned and salted fish to fresh fish. The co-op, meanwhile, lacked the capital and organizational ability to modernize its operations. The availability of unemployment insurance deterred fishermen from working for as long as they had in the past, when their livelihood depended on their catches. The educational component of the co-operative ventures fell by the wayside, and Father Forest apparently never became very good at delegating authority: "I…unfortunately have to take all responsibility in all co-operative activities locally." Consolidation of the fisheries through Guysborough Co-operative Fisheries in 1960 did not save them. This venture was taken over by a large company in 1968, the same year the Ideal Cooperative Society closed its doors. Better roads made it easier for the people of Larry's River to shop in larger centres.

This analysis of the failure of the Antigonish Movement in one small community ignores how it influenced the participants. As one person put it, "It doesn't give us only dollars and cents. It teaches us to trust one another ... to transact business with one another and best of all it teaches us to live in peace and harmony with one another." Social movements pass away. Organizations and structures crumble. But those involved in them move on to new lives, inspired by the enduring power of their leaders to transform humans. These transformations are difficult to measure, but very real.

The credit union in Larry's River gave up its charter in 1990, but the overall movement is stronger than ever in eastern Nova Scotia and a vital part of urban and rural life. In moves that would have delighted Coady, credit unions bought two branches of the National Bank in Nova Scotia in the early years of the 21st century. When banks in three communities in the province closed in 2001, credit unions moved in and set up operations. On Isle Madame in Cape Breton, 3,600 of 4,200 residents belong to the credit union, which was founded in 1937. When the cod fishery collapsed in the 1990s, the credit union became a vital backer of new business enterprises.

In 1995, Rusty Neal, a university professor, claimed that the Antigonish Movement did not extend equality to women in either philosophy or practice. Her doctoral dissertation became the book *Brotherhood Economics*, published in 1998. In a review of this work in *The Atlantic Co-operator* of June/July 1995, Jack Quarter, another academic, reinforced her claim. It brought an instant rebuttal in the next issue of the publication from Peggy MacIsaac, who had worked for four directors of St. F.X.'s Extension Department. She pointed out that Coady made a special effort to recruit women to carry out the work of the movement. And these women, some of whom I knew, always spoke warmly of the man who made such a difference in their lives. As Sister Irene Doyle, the last surviving member (in 2004) of that fine group put it, "It was fun!"

From time to time, efforts have been made to revive the Antigonish Movement. But without a leader like Moses Coady, such attempts smack of staging *Hamlet* without the Prince of Denmark. Each year, St. F.X. hosts the Topshee Conference, named for a successor to Coady who headed the Extension Department. It attracts hundreds of activists who sit and talk and talk and talk. In 1985, Dan MacInnes, a sociology professor at St. F.X. who wrote his doctoral dissertation on the Antigonish Movement, upset conference participants – and the university hierarchy – with a blunt statement:

The focused vision and social critique of the once famed Antigonish Movement has virtually disappeared from the public life. It has become the most dangerous of all Celtic mythic creatures – a live ghost.

You don't have to worry about dead ghosts. They won't bother you. Live ghosts embodied in myths keep popping up, tapping you on the shoulder, reminding you of what they achieved in the past – and demanding to know why you don't go forth and do likewise.

This mythic Celtic creature haunts adult educator Anne Alexander's *The Antigonish Movement: Moses Coady and Adult Education Today*, published in 1997. She aimed to send out a rallying cry to her fellows, hoping to energize them by recalling a dynamic part of their heritage. Alexander discovered the movement during graduate study in social work and involvement in community and international development. In a chapter entitled "Taking the Fire or Scattering the Ashes," she examines the tensions between personal advancement in adult education and community empowerment. Social movements are subversive because they criticize the traditional ways of meeting human needs by the state and the private sector, offering an alternative through which ordinary people can become masters of their own destinies. They may not achieve this goal, but they prepare the way for others seeking to make a better life through their own efforts. Alexander sought to revive what Coady modestly called "my stuff" to prevent adult education "from serving as a middle-class ghetto." Adult educators, she writes, "can develop a vision of a more humane and just society and through [our] efforts, initiate movements in this direction." She notes,

> There, in non-governmental organizations, small voluntary groups, church-sponsored projects, and cross-cultural learner centres (to mention only some examples), we can find educators of adults committed to the values and practice Coady advocated and who also have lifestyles to match.

A Man for All Times and All Places

> What will survive of us is love
>
> —Philip Larkin, "An Arundel Tomb"

Moses Coady left a powerful impression on all he encountered. His memory and the stories of what he achieved still have power to move and inspire people. In the early 1970s, I took students from the Coady International Institute, where I taught from 1971 to 1973, to Saint John,

New Brunswick. We met an elderly man who lamented, "I wish now we had paid more attention to Coady when he came here."

Kathy Bardswick, CEO of The Cooperators, recalls her mother's enthusiasm for and commitment to the idea of the co-operative as a social good, not just an economic institution. Kathy's maternal grandfather had been a founding member of the first credit union on Cape Breton. She remembers visiting a credit union and seeing a picture of her grandfather on the wall. She realized that the ideal of a community coming together to deal with life's challenges went back a long way. The company she heads has been designated as one of the best places to work in Canada.

Since its establishment in 1959, the Coady International Institute has helped over 4,700 students from over 130 countries learn how to do community-based development more effectively. These learners come from grassroots settings. They visit Coady's birthplace in the Margaree, which is still inhabited by his family members, and see the rural land in which the Antigonish Movement began. After their time at the institute, the students leave transformed and inspired. Coady's story touched and motivated a Ghanaian: "[It] reminds me that I can make a difference, and that I can help people take responsibility for their own future. It is a great inspiration."

In October 2003, I travelled to Lesotho in southern Africa to explore learning needs in community-based development. There I worked with Father Joseph Brossard, an Oblate missionary, and Anthony Setsabi, the director of a leadership program. Both had attended the Coady International Institute, caught the spirit of the Antigonish Movement and carried its fire back to Lesotho. That country, like many southern African nations, has numerous problems. Life, as it was in Nova Scotia in the 1930s, is very basic. Many people live close to the bone, struggling daily simply to survive. One third of Lesotho's population is infected with HIV/AIDS. Rural poverty, a desiccated countryside slashed by *dongas* (deep ravines) and a fragile infrastructure add to the precariousness of life. Government business ventures have been privatized and thousands of workers laid off. Taiwanese entrepreneurs own factories making jeans for North American markets, but no Basotho have been trained to manage them. This so-called Kingdom in the Clouds, with a proud history of resisting foreign invasion, has been the site of several top-down, large-scale efforts, most of which have failed, that were launched to better the lot of its people.

Father Brossard, who arrived in Lesotho in 1950, started a faculty of science and agriculture at Pius XII University, now the National University of Lesotho. Realizing very quickly that the university needed a department of adult education, he attended one of the first courses at Coady International Institute in 1960. He saw the relevance of the Antigonish Movement to Lesotho, which became independent in 1966. As he put it, "I am deeply convinced that Moses Coady was both a genius and a saint." The priest recruited twelve families to go to Lesotho to use the Antigonish approach in setting up a department of adult education at the university. As he tells the story,

> Co-operative tractor plowing projects, low income housing, small industries, upgrading of small businesses, etc. was and still is the Antigonish Movement spreading like Pentecost Fire adapting to modern social, economic and spiritual realities.

Travelling with him and listening to him, I was struck by his resemblance to what I'd heard about Moses Coady.

Energetic, abrasive, enthusiastic, with numerous contacts, the *fau fau* (the tall one) nagged at people to act. He introduced me to those who were doing so at the community level. At the age of 79, he retained the fire and stamina of a young man. So it must have been with Coady. Identifying potential leaders, he sent them to study at Coady International Institute. Anthony Setsabi, once a herd boy in the mountains, was one of these. He became a teacher and a volunteer adult educator, recruited by Brossard. He complements the priest in a quiet way, and has something of Coady's charisma. We went to a meeting of volunteers in the small community of Quithing. They were sharing what little they had with HIV/AIDS sufferers. We sang and prayed and heard presentations while Setsabi gave them words of encouragement. I felt as if I had stepped back in time, into a community meeting in Coady's early days.

Setsabi brought together the university's Institute of Extra Mural Studies and the Lesotho Christian Council of Churches. He gained the support of the Kellogg Foundation to join the Leadership Regional Network for Southern Africa (LEARN), which nurtures leadership for social and economic development in Lesotho and other countries in southern Africa. The spirit of the Antigonish Movement inspires its activities. Brossard states that the movement is still very much alive and strong internationally. He has travelled the world and seen what people at the grassroots are doing to become masters of their own destiny, despite great obstacles.

In a thesis submitted to the University of Pittsburgh, Setsabi outlined what happened after the initial burst of co-operative energy hit Lesotho. Focusing on agriculture in the Roma Valley near the university, and low-cost housing in Maseru, the capital, Brossard and his Canadian and Lesotho colleagues made great gains. The priest secured support, and funds from a wide range of sources. By May 1968, 38 credit unions with 10,000 members had been formed and a national organization established.

The co-operative movement suffered from a lack of grassroots leadership, inadequate membership participation, shortage of capital and well-intentioned government interference. At the university, the approach used by the Antigonish Movement came in conflict with the British tradition of adult education, which concerned itself with personal improvement rather than community social and economic development. The university hierarchy did not see grassroots work as the right kind of task for the institution. It concentrated resources on training an elite to take over from the departing British. They learned a lot of theory, but very little about practical ways of improving the lives of the people of Lesotho. They moved from university to government with heads full of abstract ideas, natural prey to ideologies imported from outside the country. The university library has a complete collection of Lenin's works, but very little on community development. Adult educators without degrees did not fit into academic categories. As Setsabi notes, by 1972 the Antigonish Movement philosophy had vanished from the university campus.

On my visit to Lesotho, I found ample evidence that, if the national university had lost the art of dynamic adult education, it remained alive and well among the Basotho. In Liphiring, a strong village committee set up a health clinic, improved the water supply and the schools and established a skills centre with a solar-powered computer whose excellence had been recognized by the United Nations. At Teyateyaneng, unemployed women created their own weaving venture after being laid off by a private company. On one evening, Father Brossard, Anthony Setsabi, university staff and a Maseru businessman sat together and, in an hour, worked out the idea for Lesotho's first community economic development corporation, modelled on Cape Breton's New Dawn. We called it Sunrise and prayed together for its success.

My presentations on community economic development were very well received by business people, government ministers, academics, civil servants and members of nongovernmental organizations. I pointed out that the World Bank now favoured small-scale, bottom-up, community-driven economic ventures after so many large-scale ones had failed. The language that marked the Antigonish Movement – local empowerment, community self-reliance, self-help and mutual aid – has become current again.

Coady recognized that development began in the hearts of men and women. Until they infused what they did with spirituality, nothing of lasting value resulted. F. Von Pilis, a Saskatchewan journalist, identified the driving force in Coady's life in an obituary in *The Union Farmer* of August 1959: "Love was the power motivating Dr. Coady – love of God and his fellow men."

The priest based his movement on hard economic and social common sense. But underpinning its activities was the practice of *agape*, lovingkindness. In our *eros*-saturated times, with their narcissism, celebrity worship and information overload, with most people committed to doing their own thing, *agape* can easily be confused with sloppy sentimentality. It's a hard taskmaster, demanding compassion for all – even those you consider unworthy of it.

Ida Delaney recalled her boss who never acted like a boss: "Nobody could set limits to the good that had blessed mankind because of what he had done for people whom he loved and in whom he had such great faith."

You cannot program *agape* into a plan or insert it into a vision or mission statement. It has to be lived to be real, and Coady showed how this could be done. His times were tougher than any we shall ever know. Coady's life, and those of the men and women who worked with him, stand as enduring testimonies to the power of *agape* and of tough-minded, realistic ways to tackle problems of dependency, poverty and preventable human misery. Through this transcendental force, the members of the Antigonish Movement brought hope to communities lost in despair.

Agape remains a power in the world, open and available to all who seek to follow the paths blazed by Coady and his people through the wildernesses of the oppressive forces of their time. They worked with compassion and passion, overcoming impossible odds because they believed that ordinary people had the capacity to improve their lives through their own efforts. By working together, by overcoming the fears in their own beings and in the outside world, by courage and organization, they could transform themselves, and their communities, and perhaps, just perhaps, redeem a troubled and chaotic world.

This is the living legacy of Moses Coady.

Bibliography

Alexander, Anne. *The Antigonish Movement: Moses Coady and Adult Education Today*. Toronto: Thompson Educational Publishing, 1997.

Boudreau, Alexandre J. *À l'assaut des défis*. Moncton: Les Éditions d'Acadie, 1994.

Boyle, George. *Father Tompkins of Nova Scotia*. New York: P.J. Kenedy and Sons, 1953.

Cameron, James D. *For the People: A History of St. Francis Xavier University*. Montreal and Kingston: McGill-Queen's University Press, 1996.

————. *"And Martha Served": History of the Sisters of St. Martha*. Halifax: Nimbus, 2000.

Campbell, Douglas F. *Banking on Coal: Perspectives on a Cape Breton Community within an International Context*. Sydney, NS: UCCB Press, 1997.

Cape Breton's Magazine. "With Alex John Boudreau, Chéticamp Island," No. 32 (Interview).

Chiasson, Père Anselme. *Chéticamp: Histoire et traditions acadiennes*. Moncton: Éditions des Aboiteaux, 1972.

————, ed. *L'histoire des tapis 'hookés' de Chéticamp et de leurs artisans*. Yarmouth, NS: Les Éditions Lescarbot, n.d.

Christie, Nancy, and Michael Gauvreau. *A Full-Orbed Christianity: The Protestant Churches and Social Welfare in Canada, 1900–1940*. Montreal and Kingston: McGill-Queen's University Press, 1996.

Coady, M.M. *Masters of Their Own Destiny: The Story of the Antigonish Movement of Adult Education through Economic Co-operation*. New York: Harper and Bros., 1939.

Conrad, Margaret R. and James K. Hiller. *Atlantic Canada: A Region in the Making*. Don Mills, ON: Oxford University Press, 2001.

Corbett, E.A. *We Have with Us Tonight*. Toronto: Ryerson Press, 1957.

Crerar, Duff. *Padres in No Man's Land: Canadian Chaplains and the Great War*. Montreal and Kingston: McGill-Queen's University Press, 1995.

Daly, Margaret. *The Revolution Game: The Short, Unhappy Life of the Company of Young Canadians*. Toronto: New Press, 1970.

Delaney, Ida. *By Their Own Hands: A Fieldworker's Account of the Antigonish Movement*. Hantsport, NS: Lancelot Press, 1985.

Doyle, Sister Irene. "Women of the Antigonish Movement," a talk to the Atlantic Institute, Halifax, July 21, 1982.

Elliott, C. Russell. *The Briefcase Boys: Reflections of a Church Activist*. Hantsport, NS: Lancelot Press, 1996.

Faris, Ron. *The Passionate Educators: Voluntary Associations and the Struggle for Control of Adult Education Broadcasting in Canada, 1919–1952*. Toronto: Peter Martin Assoc., 1975.

Feltmate, Peggy. "Father Jimmy, Billy Tom and the Antigonish Movement." *Early Canadian Life*, September 1980, 84–85.

Ferguson, Norman H. *The Story of the Nova Scotia Teachers' Union: From the Formation of the Old Union in 1895 to the 1980s*. Armdale, NS: Nova Scotia Teachers' Union, 1990.

Fowler, Bertram B. *The Lord Helps Those... How the People of Nova Scotia Are Solving Their Problems through Co-operation*. New York: Vanguard Press, 1938.

Haley, Stefan. *Tested by Fire: The Life and Work of W.H. McEwen*. Saskatoon: Co-operative College of Canada, 1980.

Harris, Richard. "Flattered but Not Imitated: Co-operative Self-Help and the Nova Scotia Housing Commission, 1936–1973." *Acadiensis* 31(1):103–128, Autumn 2001.

Hart, John. *History of Northeast Margaree*. Privately printed, n.p. 1963.

Hawkins, John. *The Life and Times of Angus L.* Windsor, NS: Lancelot Press, 1969.

Hobsbawn, Eric. *Age of Extremes: The Short Twentieth Century, 1914–1991*. London: Abacus, 1995.

Hutten, Anne. *Valley Gold: The Story of the Apple Industry in Nova Scotia*. Halifax: Petheric Press, 1981.

Jamieson, Patrick. "Antigonish: The Two-Sided Legacy," in Ian McKay and Scott Milsom, *Toward a New Maritimes*. Charlottetown, PEI: Ragweed Press, 1992.

Laidlaw, Alexander F. *Campus and Community: The Global Impact of the Antigonish Movement.* Montreal: Harvest House, 1961.

————. *The Man from Margaree: Writings and Speeches of M.M. Coady.* Toronto: Mc-Clelland and Stewart, 1971.

————. "The Coady-Tompkins Experience." Remarks at the Coady-Tompkins Symposium, Scarboro Foreign Mission Society, Scarborough, Ontario, March 10-11, 1978.

Leadbeater, Charles. *The Rise of the Social Entrepreneur.* London: Demos, 1997.

Lotz, Jim. "The Antigonish Movement: A Critical Analysis." *Studies in Adult Education,* 5(2):97–112, 1973.

————. "The Historical and Social Setting of the Antigonish Movement." *Nova Scotia Historical Quarterly* 52(2):99–116, 1975.

————. *Understanding Canada.* Toronto: NC Press, 1977.

————. "Hope in a Time of Despair: A Lesotho Story." *Catholic New Times,* January 4, 2004, 8.

————. "From Antigonish to Africa: Atlantic Ideas Spurring Change in Troubled Nation." *The Atlantic Co-operator,* February 2004, 2–3.

————. "Weaving New Lives in Africa." *Nova Scotia Craft News,* Winter 2004, 8.

Lotz, Jim and Michael R. Welton. " 'Knowledge for the People': The Origins and Development of the Antigonish Movement," in Michael Welton, ed., *Knowledge for the People.* Toronto: OISE Press, 1987.

————. *Father Jimmy: The Life and Times of Jimmy Tompkins.* Wreck Cove, NS: Breton Books, 1997.

Lotz, Patricia. *Scots in Groups: The Origin and History of Scottish Societies with Particular Reference to Those Established in Nova Scotia.* MA Thesis (Celtic Studies). St. Francis Xavier University, 1975.

————. "The History of Library Development in the Atlantic Provinces," in Lorraine Spencer and Carl Garry, eds., *Canadian Libraries in Their Changing Environment.* Toronto: York University Centre for Continuing Education, 1977.

Lotz, Pat and Jim Lotz. *Cape Breton Island.* Vancouver: Douglas, David and Charles, 1974.

MacAulay, Scott. "The Community Economic Development Tradition in Eastern Nova Scotia, Canada: Ideological Continuities and Discontinuities between the Antigonish Movement and the Family." *Community Development Journal,* 36(2):111–121, April 2001.

MacDonald, J.D. Nelson. *Memoirs of an Unorthodox Clergyman.* Truro, NS: Cooperative Resources, 1986.

MacEachern, Allan J. "All Those Years: Practice and Purpose in Politics," in Tom Kent, ed., *In Pursuit of the Public Good: Essays in Honour of Allan J. MacEachern.* Montreal and Kingston: McGill-Queen's Press, 1997.

MacEwan, Paul. *Miners and Steelworkers: Labour in Cape Breton.* Toronto: Samuel Stevens, Hakkert and Co., 1976.

MacInnes, Daniel. "The Role of the Scottish Catholic Society in the Determination of the Antigonish Movement," *Scottish Tradition,* 7/8:24–46, 1977–78.

MacLean, Judith Flora and Daniel MacInnes. "What Can the Women Do? The Antigonish Movement and Its Programs for Women, 1918–1945." Paper presented at the University of Prince Edward Island, Charlottetown, Canadian Association for Studies in Co-operation, June 1, 1992.

MacLellan, Malcolm. *Coady Remembered.* Antigonish, NS: St. Francis Xavier University Press, 1985.

MacPherson, Ian. *Each for All: The History of the Co-operative Movement in English Canada, 1900–1945.* Toronto: Macmillan, 1979. The Carleton Library, No. 116.

———. *Co-operation, Conflict and Consensus: B.C. Central and the Credit Union Movement to 1994.* Vancouver, BC: Central Credit Union, 1995.

———. *Hands around the Globe: A History of the International Credit Union Movement and the Role and Development of the World Council of Credit Unions, Inc.* Victoria: Horsdal and Schubert, 1999.

Mathews, Race. *Jobs of Our Own: Building a Stakeholder Society – Alternatives to the Market and the State.* Annandale, Australia, and West Wickham, England: Pluto Press and Comerford and Miller, 1999.

McGowan, Mark G. "Harvesting the 'Red Vineyard': Catholic Religious Culture in the Canadian Expeditionary Force, 1914–1919." *Historical Studies* (The Canadian Catholic Historical Association), 64:47–70, 1998.

McKay, Ian. *The Quest of the Folk: Antimodernism and Cultural Selection in Twentieth Century Nova Scotia.* Montreal and Kingston: McGill-Queen's Press, 1994.

Michael, Sister Marie. "The Importance of Working with Women in the Co-operative Movement." Address given to the Staff Conference, St. Francis Xavier Extension Department, Antigonish, Nova Scotia, 1942.

———. "Women of the Antigonish Movement." Talk to the Atlantic Institute, Halifax, July 22, 1982.

National Film Board. *Moses Coady* (video), 1976.

Neal, Rusty. *Brotherhood Economics: Women and Co-operatives in Nova Scotia*. Sydney, NS: UCCB Press, 1998.

Reid, John G. *Six Crucial Decades: Times of Change in the History of the Maritimes*. Halifax: Nimbus, 1987.

Report on the Proposed Federation of the Maritime University, submitted to the Board of Governors of St. Francis Xavier College by a committee appointed by His Lordship Bishop Morrison, n.p. 1923 (?).

Report of the Royal Commission investigating the Fisheries of the Maritime Provinces and Magdalen Islands. Ottawa: King's Printer, 1928.

Report of the Royal Commission on National Development in the Arts, Letters and Sciences, 1949–51. Ottawa, King's Printer: 1951.

Ricker, Eric W., ed. *Education and Development in Atlantic Canada*. Halifax: Department of Education, Dalhousie University, 1978. "The Antigonish Movement: Perspectives and Interpretations," 163–192.

Sacoumen, E. James. "Underdevelopment and the Structural Origins of the Antigonish Movement Co-operatives in Eastern Nova Scotia," in Robert J. Brym and R. James Sacoumen, *Underdevelopment and Social Movements in Atlantic Canada*. Toronto: New Hogtown Press, 1979.

Setsabi, Anthony. *Transnational Transportation of a Social Movement: The Application of the Antigonish Movement in Lesotho*. Thesis, Graduate School of Public and International Affairs, University of Pittsburgh, 1975.

Skalicky, K. "The Catholic Church and Workers' Participation," in Jaroslav Vanek, ed., *Self-Management: Economic Liberation of Man*. Harmondsworth: Penguin, 1975.

Steele, Harvey Pablo SFM. *Winds of Change: Social Justice through Co-operatives*. Truro, NS: Co-operative Resources, 1986.

———. *Dear Old Rebel: A Priest's Battle for Social Justice*. Lawrencetown Beach, NS: Pottersfield Press, 1993.

Tompkins, Rev. Dr. J.J. *Knowledge for the People: A Call to St. Francis Xavier College*. Antigonish, NS, n.p., 1921.

Tufts, Evelyn. "The Co-operative Movement." *Canadian Geographical Journal* 21(2):99–105, August 1940.

Walsh, F. Waldo. *We Fought for the Little Man*. Moncton, NB: Co-op Atlantic, 1978.

Walsh, Patrick F. *The History of Antigonish*. Antigonish, NS: Scotia Design Publications, 1989.

Ward, Leo. *Nova Scotia: The Land of Co-operation*. New York: Sheed and Ward, 1942.

Watson, Patrick and Hugh Graham. "Moses Coady: Beyond the Mountain," in *The Canadians: Biographies of a Nation*, Vol. III. Toronto: McArthur and Co., 2002. Companion to the History Television Documentary, written and directed by Whitman Trecartin.

Welton, Michael R. "Dangerous Knowledge: Canadian Workers' Education in the Decades of Discord." *Studies in the Education of Adults*, 23(1): 24–40, April 1991.

————. "Social Revolutionary Learning: The New Social Movements as Learning Sites." *Adult Education Quarterly* 43(3):152–164, Spring 1993.

————. "Bolsheviks of a Better Sort: Jimmy Tompkins and the Struggle for a People's Catholicism, 1908–1928." *Proceedings*, Adult Education Research Conference, Edmonton, 1995.

————. *Little Mosie from Margaree: A Biography of Moses Michael Coady*. Toronto: Thompson Educational Publishers, 2001.